Now's the Day and Now's the Hour

Now's the Day and Now's the Hour

By
Carl Peterson

Dream Catcher Publishing, Inc.

Copyright 2004, Carl Peterson

All rights reserved, no part of this book may be reproduced, stored in a retrieval system, or transmitted by any means, electronic, mechanical. photocopying, recording or otherwise without written permission of the author.

ISBN: 0-9712189-7-8

Library of Congress Control Number: 2004104677

Published by

Dream Catcher Publishing, Inc.
P.O. Box 33883
Decatur, Ga. 30033
Fax: 888-771-2800
www.DreamCatcherPublishing.net

Acknowledgements

Thanks to those who helped in the research among other things and to those who offered encouragement. To Carl and Nancy Ford who made me aware of the Celtic South, Sheila Dobbie for her help in research and editing, Susan Engard for her research (and patience). To Bonnie Rideout on fiddle for her great input in the recorded CD versions and tune selections. To pipers Doug McConnell and Ian Parker and to Andy White for his drumming. Frank Vance from the Grandfather Mountain Scottish Games, Dr. Bruce Winders of The Alamo, the folks at The Library of Congress and the DRT Library at The Alamo. Also to Rennie McLeod of Unicorn Publishing for his input and Dwan Hightower for wanting to publish this book.

Book Cover

The cover uses as its background the Texas Bluebonnet tartan and the MacGregor tartan. The colours of the Texas Bluebonnet tartan, a district tartan, are based on the bluebonnet flower, which is widespread in many parts of Texas. The flower changes colour with the passing of time, the 'brim' becoming flecked with a wine red color. This tartan has been accredited by the Scottish Tartans Society.

The MacGregor tartan represents the presence of John MacGregor, a Scotchman who played the bagpipes during the siege, and sometimes tried to musically out-duel a fiddler player, who may have been Davy Crockett.

The top picture is of the Alamo and shows where the end came for some freedom fighters. The lower picture is Stirling Castle. It was in view of this castle that Scotland's freedom wars were started, with Wallace's Battle of Stirling Bridge, and Robert the Bruce's Battle of Bannockburn.

To my father Charles (Charlie) who always wanted to write a book but didn't, and to my sister Sally and my daughter Jennifer who did.

Table of Contents

Preface 1
Foreword 2
Introduction 5
A Brief History of Scotland 8
    The Highlands and The Lowlands 15
    The Massacre of Glencoe 16
    Culloden 17
    The Highland Clearances 19
Scottish Influence in American History 21
    Scottish Emigration 21
    Scotch 22
    The Scotch-Irish 24
    The Scots and the American Revolutionary Way 26
    Famous Scottish Americans 28
    Scottish Influence Found in American Documents 31
Scotland, The Alamo, and Texas 36
    Scottish Influences in Texas History 36
    A Brief History of The Alamo 37
    The Settlement of Texas 38
    Key Figures In Early Texas History 42
        Sam Houston 42
        David Crockett 44
        More on Micajah Autry 50
        John Hubbard Forsyth 50
        James Bowie 51
        William Barrett Travis 54
        Moses Rose 60
        John MacGregor 61
        Other Scots at the Alamo 62
        General Antonio López de Santa Anna 63
        Captain Ewen Cameron 64
    Influence of Sir Walter Scott, Robert Burns and Lord Byron 65
    Gringo 71
Epilogue 73

- The Songs and the Music 76
  - Remember the Alamo 77
  - Hey Tutti Taiti/ Scots Wha Ha'e 79
  - Hey Tutti Taiti 80
  - Scots Wha Ha'e 82
  - Remember the Alamo 83
  - San Jacinto 84
  - The Flowers of Edinburgh 85
  - Dashing White Sergeant 88
  - Female Volunteer for Mexico 92
  - Bugle Calls 93
  - Moses Rose of Texas 96
  - The Anacreontic Song 98
  - Death of Davy Crockett 102
  - Texas War Cry 104
  - Will You Come to the Bower 105
  - Billy Taylor 107
  - Zachary Taylor 109
  - Freedom and Texas 110
  - The Birks of Aberfeldy 112
  - Uncle Sam to Texas 113
  - Draw the Sword Scotland 115
  - To the Field, Freemen 118
  - The Union Call 119
  - All the Blue Bonnets are Over the Border 121
  - Santa Anna's March 122
  - Santa Anna's Retreat from Cerro Gordo 125
  - Auld Lang Syne 128
  - Texas Heroes 130
- The Men Who Died at the Alamo 131
- Texas History Time Line 133
- Bibliography 136

Preface

What started off as a music companion book to a double CD that I had recorded of period music from the Southern states and early Texas, ended up being a sort of history book. I realized that calling a double CD "Scotland Remembers the Alamo" needed some explanation. We seem to forget that early Americans were not that far removed from the countries of their origin. Some were new immigrants while the ones who were born in America still had close ties to the countries and the cultures of their forefathers. Different nationalities tended to form their own communities. In those early days there was nothing much to assimilate into, so those communities would tend to carry on the cultures of their origins. Thus, among other things, the music and stories and their histories would play a large part in the everyday lives of these people.

When I learned there had been a bagpiper who had died at the Alamo and a fiddle player who played Scottish tunes, I was compelled to find out what other music would have been played and sung at that time. I went back to early American song books and found that most of the music was music they brought with them from the their own countries. When events happened they would use these same tunes to write new songs. Identifying the songs with the people would identify them with their past and explain how they handled things in the present and into the future. When faced with the situation in Texas the settlers handled it the same way as their forefathers would have. It was a fight against tyranny and for freedom, that their forefathers had been fighting for centuries. Most of these early settlers were Scottish or of Scottish origin and their fight against tyranny and for freedom goes back to the 11th and 12th centuries, to the days of William Wallace and Robert the Bruce. The music and the songs from that time period proves the knowledge of these days and throughout Scottish history. Knowing this, one understands better the fight the Alamo defenders put up against the tyranny of Santa Anna. For some of them it was a fight that their fathers and grandfathers had experienced during the American Revolution against Britain.

Foreword

The story of the Alamo has always held a special fascination for me. It started when I was a boy growing up in Scotland and went to see Walt Disney's *Davy Crockett* in the cinema. Later a group known as the Kingston Trio recorded a song called "Remember The Alamo". Then along came John Wayne's version of *The Alamo*. This was how we learned American history, from American movies, the cowboys and Indians, movies of the old West, gangster movies showing the Great American cities of New York and Chicago. The history we learned in school was of course Scottish history, especially of William Wallace and Robert the Bruce and the conflicts through the centuries between England and Scotland. We celebrated Scotland's victories and we mourned her losses. I little realized while I was learning about William Wallace and Robert the Bruce that countless generations before me had learned the same, and they would take the stories of Scotland's successes to every corner of the world where Scots had migrated. Hence it was not until many years later that I realized that the fight at the Alamo was one of Scottish spirit and independence against a tyrant who threatened the freedom and independence of the settlers of early Texas.

For me it really just started as a vague wondering of why 200 or so men would be so willing to stand up against a force of close to 3000 soldiers. They seemed to realize through the 13-day siege that they were bound to die and yet seemed bound and determined to meet their fate with uncanny bravery. I realized later of course that many miscalculations led to their predicament and there was not much choice but to do what they did, but somehow there seemed to be more to it than just that, and there was.

The rebirth of my interest started in the late 1980s when I was touring and singing at colleges and schools in the Midwest. I was flying from Philadelphia to Wichita, Kansas and, as I was flipping through the in-flight magazine, I ran across an article about a large Scottish gathering and festival in Texas. The article went on to mention that such a large gathering of Scots in Texas was not unusual, for the Scots had a huge part in the early history of the Southern states and particularly Texas and that indeed four Scots died at the Alamo including a piper called John MacGregor who played his pipes while a fiddler, who some claim was Davy Crockett, played his fiddle. This fiddler, whoever he was, was also known to have played Scottish tunes at the Alamo. Indeed a majority of the Alamo defenders were of Scotch-Irish ancestry. This was a term that I had not been familiar with until I came to United States. The term used in Britain was Ulster Scots.

What led me to believe that this was a very Scottish influenced affair was the music and the songs of those times. For myself, the music identified the people more than anything else I had run across before this. I was already familiar with the song "Remember The Alamo" written by Jane Bowers and recorded by the Kingston Trio in the 1950s but I was curious about what tunes piper MacGregor might have played or what tunes the fiddler fiddled to keep the men in good spirits. The best place to go, I was told, was the Library of Congress (LOC) or the Daughters of the Republic of Texas library at the Alamo. Off I went to the music department of the LOC and looked up everything with the word Alamo. I uncovered a wealth of information including Alamo songs and also old music books published back then that indicated the popular songs and music of those times. Most of the material was Scottish, English or Irish and that any American songs in these books although not many, were written to Scottish, English or Irish tunes. I soon realized that America, being a young country, had not yet entirely developed its own character and that American lifestyles were still somewhat similar to those in the Old Country. Gaelic was being spoken as a first language in many southern communities and Scottish and English accents were still prevalent and had not yet evolved into American dialects. They maintained their British ways and sense of history and old animosities. Some old fights were still going on. Times would change soon enough and Sam Houston in his old age would remark that American authors would not need to look to "European castles and their crazy knights and lady loves" but "set themselves to work to glean the unwritten legends of heroism and adventures which the old men would tell them who are now smoking their pipes around the rooftrees of Kentucky and Tennessee." But Sam Houston in his younger days would look to Scottish history and Robert Burns' poetry to inspire himself and his army to victory against Mexico. This is not surprising, for Sam Houston himself was of Scottish ancestry.

On October 2nd 1835 Mexican soldiers were ordered to retrieve a cannon from the town of Gonzales but were prevented by the townsfolk from doing so. This was the Texas version of "the shot heard around the world" and although many knew it was inevitable, The Texas Revolution had started. At 11pm Friday evening, October 2nd, Sam Houston, as "Commander-in-Chief of the forces," for the district of Nacogdoches scattered an appeal for volunteers which started thus:

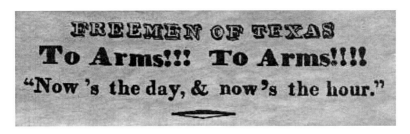

The last line of the headline is of course from Robert Burns' poem "Scots Wha Ha'e", originally entitled "Bruce's Address to his Troops before Bannockburn." It would not be the last time Houston would quote Burns. It would certainly be one of many times that Burns' music and words would be used socially and inspirationally to write songs of Texas. The writings of another popular Scottish poet and author, Sir Walter Scott, would figure prominently as did the writings of George Gordon Byron (Lord Byron) who was brought up in Aberdeen, Scotland by his Scottish mother and who called himself "half a Scot and bred a whole one". The primary reason for this book is to demonstrate through the music how important the Scottish spirit was in Texas and at the Alamo. When you understand the history then you understand the music, for the music connects the people to their culture, present and past, which, in this case, illustrates a people fighting for survival against tyranny and oppression.

Introduction

Thomas Babington Macaulay, in the introduction to his *History of England*, wrote: "I should very improperly execute the task which I have undertaken if I were merely to treat of battles and sieges, of the rise and fall of administrations, or intrigues in the palace and debates in the parliament. It will be my endeavor to relate the history of the people as well as the history of the government, to trace the progress of useful and ornamental arts, to describe the rise of religious sects and the changes of literary taste, to portray the manners of successive generations, I'm not to pass by with neglect even the revolutions which have taken place in the dress, furniture, repasts and public amusements. I shall cheerfully hear the reproach of having descended below the dignity of history, if I can succeed in placing before the England of the 19th-century the true picture of the life of our ancestors."

For "England of the 19th-century" read, "Texas of the 19th-century" and you have, more or less, the points and object of this book. For the people of the early United States, particularly those who went to Texas, and particularly those who fought and died in the Alamo, their past history and the history of their forefathers cannot be ignored. It is therefore necessary that we should recognize and take into account why these immigrants, sons of immigrants, grandsons of immigrants, went to America and Texas to find a new way of life and why they were willing to fight to the death to preserve that new way of life. It is not only necessary to remember the dates and the places of events and the leaders, but of the many individuals who took part. They came with a knowledge of who their forefathers were, and this knowledge influenced their character, actions and way of life.

Sam Houston once wrote to a correspondent, "Bear in mind that all histories from the Rock of Plymouth, and Jamestown to the present time, have been made by white men, and a man who tells his own story, is always right until the adversary's tale is told." In any critical age of revolt by any human groups who have been passive, too many wrongs have been done. The Scots, in their Declaration of Arbroath speak of their journey "from Greater Scythia by way of the Tyrrhenian Sea…to their home in the west where they still live today. The Britons they first drove out, the Picts they utterly destroyed ... And took possession of that home with many victories." The American Declaration of Independence tells of "the merciless Indian Savages, whose known rule of warfare, is an undistinguished destruction of all ages, sexes and condition." Yet these Britons, Picts and native American Indians were being encroached upon by invaders.

I am reminded of a French humorist who, two centuries ago, published "La Menagerie" in which there is illustrated a caged animal with the notice, "This animal is very mischievous, when attacked it defends itself". So indeed was Mexico. It had barely won its independence from Spain when its own immigration laws were being violated, but then again so too were the legal rights of the settlers under the Constitution of 1824. The situation produced a tyrant which both Texians and Mexicans had to deal with, and as a result, Mexico lost Texas in a fight for freedom from tyranny.

> "Let there be light!" said God and there was light,
> "Let there be blood!" said man, and there's a sea.
> -Byron

So, before we go a little way back, it is necessary to go a long way back, and this we will do. We will go back to the 11th and 12th centuries, to the days of William Wallace and Robert the Bruce and their fight for independence and freedom, to the Jacobite wars of the 1700s, to the union of the crowns and the union of the governments and to the many fights against tyrants and oppressive kings and governments.

Practically every generation of Scots had learned of the bravery of William Wallace and Robert the Bruce and indeed evidence suggests that the men of the Alamo fought with a knowledge of this history and they likened their fight against Santa Anna and the Mexican forces to the fight of Wallace and Bruce against Edward I and Edward II and their vast English armies. William Barrett Travis, the commander of the Alamo forces, might even have likened his fight to that of the Scottish Jacobites, led by Bonnie Prince Charles Edward Stuart against a Hanoverian government.

Reader, let us then proceed.

A Brief History of Scotland

Perhaps it is better first to mention some of the most important dates in Scotland's history, for these are the dates that influenced the future of Scotland and indeed the future of the countries Scots would emigrate to. The first date would have to be Wallace's victory at Stirling Bridge, September 11, 1297, the first major battle in Scotland's freedom wars against Edward I and English dominance. Next would be The Battle of Bannockburn, June 23-24 in 1314, another major step for freedom with Robert The Bruce this time leading the Scots against Edward II. In 1603 James VI of Scotland would become James I of England thus uniting the British crowns, a triumph for a Scot where so many English kings had failed. The treachery of the King and government against the Highlanders of Glencoe, February 13, 1692, The Union of the Governments in 1707, the defeat of Bonnie Prince Charles Edward Stuart and his Highland army at Culloden, April 16th in 1746, and finally the start of the Highland Clearances in 1792 would all bring major changes to Scotland and to lands where Scots would migrate. To the reader I will attempt to demonstrate how these events would influence America, especially the Southern states, Texas and the Alamo. We must first go a little bit further back to set the scene in Scotland leading up to these events.

Around 843 A.D. Kenneth MacAlpin became King of the Picts and Scots. He died in A.D. 858 and was succeeded by his brother Donald I. The first monarch to be called king of Scotland was Donald II around 889 A.D.

In 1237 the Treaty of York fixed the Scottish border with England. Scotland at that time was under the reign of Alexander II. In 1249 came the death of Alexander II and the accession of Alexander III to the throne at the age of eight years. Two years later, on December 25, 1251, Alexander III married Princess Margaret, sister of Edward I of England. Princess Margaret was eight years old, married to the 10-year-old king of Scotland. By the time she died in 1275, at the age of 35, Alexander and Margaret had three children. Six years later David, her second son, died as did her daughter, giving birth to another Margaret. By January 1284 Alexander's only surviving son, Lord Alexander died and the only heir to the throne was Alexander's granddaughter in Norway, Princess Margaret, known as "The Maid of Norway" the daughter of Eric II of Norway and Alexander's daughter Margaret. She was proclaimed heir and in October 1285 Alexander III remarried. His new bride, Yolande of Dreux, was French. On March 19, 1286, after a meeting with his council, Alexander was riding from Edinburgh to Fife to be with his French bride. It was a stormy night and he apparently crossed the Firth of Forth safely but lost his escort on the shores of Fife, his horse stumbled in the dark and the King fell. His broken body was found below the cliffs the next morning. The stumbling of the King's horse at Kinghorn could be viewed as the greatest calamity ever to happen to Scotland. The country was plunged into confusion and eventual civil war over who was to rule Scotland. Six "Guardians of the Realm" were appointed, the Maid of Norway was accepted as queen and arrangements were made to have her returned to Scotland. Robert de Bruce, a baron and Lord of Annandale, maintained it was not lawful for a woman to sit on the throne and claimed he was rightful heir. He raised a large army of support including several nobles and seized several strongholds in the south. But Edward I then counseled that his son should wed Margaret, providing Scotland with a king. It seemed a favorable plan to the regents but came to an end when word reached Scotland that young Margaret had died on her way from Norway. Scotland now had an empty throne with thirteen claimants. Civil war loomed on the horizon but a possible solution seemed to be the appointment of an arbiter and with the consent of all parties concerned, Edward I was chosen with the condition that all claimants would recognize the right of the English throne to suzerainty over Scotland. Every one of them agreed and Edward chose John de Baliol as his puppet king. To his credit, Baliol did eventually renounce his homage and looked to France for help by forming a defensive and offensive alliance in 1295 known as the Auld Alliance. It was a treaty drawn up by the French monarch Philip IV and John Baliol aimed at Edward I. There may have been earlier precedent but this was the first documented evidence of such a treaty.

The start of the dispute for the throne of Scotland started in 1286 with the death of Alexander III and the interference by Edward I of England.

Edward I and Alexander III as far as history shows had been personal friends and had acted as independent kings but Edward always thought that the kingship of Scotland was subject to the crown of England. He searched every possible document in England to prove his claim by establishing many instances of homage paid by Scottish kings to England over hundreds of years. The "high men" of Scotland were challenged to disprove his claims but before long Edward had taken control of the situation as English overlord and made his terms very clear. According to Edward there was a Scotland but not a Kingdom of Scotland, but not according to the Scots, as Edward was soon to find out.

The flame of patriotism and the fight for freedom was led by common Scots, not nobility, for the nobles were foreigners, most of whom had lands in England for which they owed their fealty to the English king. William Wallace was the leader of the common Scots, a man of quick and passionate temper and a deep and early hatred of the English. He raised a band of common Scots around him of similar sentiment, his army quickly increased and Scotland's fight for freedom had started. Wallace was not just a guerrilla fighter and not just a leader of a patriotic movement, but a man of spirit and of vision who communicated with European cities inviting exchange of trade for Scotland. Some of the nobility, seeing Wallace's growing success, began to come to his side. An English chronicler would write "the whole of the followers of the nobility had attached themselves to him, and, although the persons of their lords were with the king of England, their hearts were with Wallace, who found his army reinforced by so immense a multitude of the Scots that the community of the land obeyed him as their leader and their prince." He would become Sir William Wallace and guardian of Scotland and one of his crowning achievements during this fight for Scottish freedom came on September 11, 1297 in what would become known as the Battle of Stirling Bridge. Edward sent an army to Scotland and Wallace was more than ready to give him battle. John de Warenne, the Earl Surrey, was in charge of the English army and did try to come to terms with the Scots by sending two friars to parley with Wallace but Scotland's freedom was not to be bargained for. Wallace's reply was "Return to your friends and tell them that we came with no peaceful intent, but ready for battle, and determined to avenge our own wrongs and set our country free. Let your masters come and attack us; we are ready to meet them beard to beard." The Scottish army was said to consist of 40,000 foot and 180 horse while the English force was made up of 50,000 foot and 1,000 horse. Separating the armies was a wooden bridge, so narrow that only two horses at a time could cross and, unknown to the English army, had been weakened by the Scots. When half the English army had crossed, the bridge was sent crashing, which split their army in two. The Scots attacked with a vengeance, giving no quarter, their only intent was to kill, taking no prisoners. This victory would certainly revive the spirit of freedom and independence in the more common folk, the real Scots, but treachery in the Scottish nobility and Edward's loyal Scottish followers betrayed Wallace. They were mostly Normans whose families had not been long in Scotland, who owned land in England and could change loyalties however it suited them. Though much success followed Wallace's victory at Stirling, his army was defeated near Falkirk on July 22nd, 1298 and Edward once more gained dominance.

England and France made peace on May 20, 1303 leaving Scotland in the cold and nullifying the treaty of 1295. Baliol had given up his crown in 1296 and the guardianship of Scotland was given over to the Earl of Surrey. The nullification allowed Edward to continue his campaign against Scotland without worrying about France, and he gradually took control of Scotland. The last castle to fall into his hands was Stirling Castle on the July 20, 1304. Wallace did not submit but continued his guerrilla campaigns until August 3, 1305 when he was betrayed, captured and turned over to the English by Sir John Menteith. On the 23rd he was tried, condemned to death and hanged, drawn and quartered as a traitor to the King of England. Wallace's violent and brutal execution earned contempt for the English king in Scotland and his death was burned into the Scottish spirit.

Around 1477 a poet known as Blind Harry wrote *The Wallace*, an epic poem in the Northern English language (Lallans) that became one of the first books printed in Scotland (about 1508). In 1722 poet William Hamilton of Gilbertfield translated and adapted Blind Harry's poem and this version became the most commonly owned book in Scotland next to the Bible. Ann Grant, who came to America from Scotland in 1758 at the age of three, when her father was an officer in the 55th regiment of the British army, mentions having it read to her during her stay in the Colonies. After her return to Scotland, she became a famous author, recalling a lot of her American experiences in her *Memoirs Of An American Lady*.

Jane Porter (1776-1850), borrowing from Blind Harry, wrote the story of Wallace in novel form published in 1809 as *The Scottish Chiefs*. It has been translated into Russian, German and French. Modern audiences will have learned about William Wallace through a Hollywood movie called *Braveheart* starring Mel Gibson as Wallace. *The Wallace* influenced Robert Burns, Lord Byron and William Wordsworth among others. Burns wrote "...the story of Wallace poured a Scottish prejudice in my veins which will boil along there until the floodgates of life shut in eternal rest." When Burns wrote out the text of "Robert Bruce's Address to his Army at Bannockburn" (Scots Wha Ha'e) he borrowed from William Hamilton's version of Blind Harry's poem:
"a false usurper sinks in ev'ry foe,
And liberty returns with every blow."

Burns wrote:
Tyrants fall in every foe
Liberty's in every blow!

The start of Hamilton's *Wallace* reads thus:
Of our ancestors, brave true ancient Scots,
Whose glorious scutcheons knew no bars nor blots;
But blood untainted circled ev'ry vein,
And ev'ry thing ignoble did disdain;
Of such illustrious patriots and bold,
Who stoutly did maintain our rights of old,
Who their malicious, and invet'rate foes,
With sword in hand, did gallantly oppose:
And in their own, and nations just defense,

Did briskly check the frequent insolence
Of haughty neighbors, enemies profest,
Picts, Danes, and Saxons, Scotland's very pest;
Of such, I say, I'll brag and vaunt so long
As I have pow'r to use my pen or tongue;
And sound their praises in such modern strain,
As suiteth best a Scot's poetic vein.

Wallace's death did not end Scotland's fight for freedom and independence, it was just the beginning. John Baliol, who had been king, was no longer in the picture and the main contenders were Robert the Bruce and John Comyn. On February 10, 1306 a meeting was arranged with Bruce and Comyn in the Greyfriars Church in Dumfries, and in what was considered by most historians to be premeditated murder, Bruce stabbed Comyn at the altar. Edward reacted by sending Comyn's brother-in-law to Scotland with orders to "burn and slay and raise dragon". The dragon emblem was a battle flag which meant that no quarter would be given.

Robert the Bruce, by his own ambition became king and was crowned at Scone in March 1306. He met his first defeat with his army on the morning of June 19, 1306 at Methven. He was now a fugitive and turned a tradition of self-serving ambition into patriotic leadership and became a well respected king. Scotland needed a king to carry on Wallace's fight and to not give up their concept of a Kingdom. People supported him not through duty but for their desire to be a free and independent nation and Bruce developed that message and led them to the cause, a cause about freedom and liberty. Like Wallace's fight it was guerrilla warfare, fast appearances and fast disappearances, until at last that decisive battle at Bannockburn.

There is an old story told of Bruce losing six battles against the English and was almost ready to give up. He was hiding in a cave and happened to notice a spider attempting to climb to his web. The spider failed six times but on the seventh try was successful. Bruce apparently saw this as a sign and in his seventh battle, which happened to be Bannockburn, he was victorious.

Edward I had died on July 7, 1307 and the throne went to his son Edward II. It was Edward II who, in 1314, brought in an army to Bannockburn. Edward's army consisted of 16,000 infantry, 2500 mounted knights and a supply train that stretched 20 miles, while Bruce had about 6000 spear men, a few archers and 500 light horse. The battle was fought over two days, June 23 and 24, and the English force was defeated. King Edward II left the field with 500 knights and although this was by no means the end of conflict between Scotland and England it confirmed Scotland as a Kingdom and independent nation. Six years later Scotland drew up what is thought to be the first declaration of independence written by any nation.

The Declaration of Arbroath was a document dated April 6, 1320 written to Pope John XXII in the name of the community of the realm, sealed by eight earls and thirty-one barons and written by the Abbot of Arbroath, Bernard Linton, in Latin. It said in part:

> …for as long as but a hundred of us shall remain alive, never will we on any conditions be brought under English rule. It is not in truth nor for glory, nor riches, nor honours that we are fighting, but for freedom---for that alone, which no honest man gives up but with his life.

On March 17, 1328 England officially recognized Scotland as a Kingdom in the Treaty of Edinburgh-Northampton.

Scotland and England would be at constant war for centuries to come but they were brought together over a period of time with the Union of the Crowns in 1603 when Elizabeth I of England died and the crown of England was taken over by James VI of Scotland who also now became known as James I of England. He was king of Scotland from 1567 to 1603 and king of Great Britain from 1603 to 1625. It was during his reign in 1610 that James started colonizing Northern Ireland with mostly Scottish lowland farmers. James was a Stewart descended from Robert I whose daughter Marjory married Walter the Steward of Scotland. Thus the line of Stewart Kings was started, though the spelling of the name would be changed to Stuart with Mary Queen of Scots coming to the throne in 1542 after the death of her father, James V. Mary had spent many years in France and the spelling of Stuart, as opposed to Stewart, was French. In 1688, the last of the Stuarts to sit on the throne, James VII, fled to France and in 1689 Parliament deposed James and claimed the right to choose the monarch. William III and Mary II were then confirmed as joint sovereigns until 1694 when the death of Mary brought sole reign to William III. Upon the death of William III in 1702 good Queen Anne ruled until her death in 1714 which brought about the accession of George I, the beginning of the Hanoverian rule. On January 16, 1707 the Scottish Parliament was dissolved and the Parliament of the United Kingdom was formed.

The Highlands and The Lowlands

Scotland through the centuries was always two different cultures, the Celtic Highlanders in the North and the Scots of Anglo-Saxon, Briton and Norman descent in the South. There has always been an imaginary line known as the Highland line or the Celtic line which runs from around Glasgow to somewhere between Aberdeen and Inverness in the Northeast of Scotland. It was given official status on the maps of Scotland in 1784 when the Wash Act was passed, an Act that for the first time drew a formal distinction between the Highlands and the Lowlands. The boundary was needed for the taxation of whisky. Highland whisky was taxed differently than Lowland whisky and was to create a legal battle which would determine what was whisky and what was not, a battle that would not be determined by the courts until 1909. Nevertheless the cultural division had been there for centuries and apart from Scotland's differences with England, Scotland itself was fractured, and many battles would be fought over the years between the Highland culture and the Lowland culture. To the people of Lowland Scotland, Highlanders were wild and savage tribesmen who kept the Lowlands in turmoil. Lowlanders hated Highlanders and Highlanders had a Gaelic expression for it, "Mi-run mor nan Gall", the "Lowlanders great hatred". Stealing cattle was a way of life and favorite pastime for the Highlanders and to live near the borders of the Highlands one had to be constantly on guard against constant raids.

The Massacre of Glencoe
Murder Under Trust

The Highland way of life had been changing over the years and some pinpoint the massacre of Glencoe as the beginning of the end for the Highlands. In 1692, the Highland clans were asked to pledge their allegiance to King William III. Many Scottish clans remained loyal to the Stuarts but in August of 1691 a truce was called in an effort to bring unity to the nation. The MacDonalds of Glencoe were late in pledging their allegiance to the King by taking their papers to the wrong location. Men in high government office, who had an intense dislike for Highlanders and in particular clan chief Alastair MacDonald, known as MacIan, and his Glencoe MacDonalds, had already decided to make an example of the clan in the pretense that it was a warning to other clans who had still not signed. MacIan was under the belief that everything was in order and that their pledge had been accepted so was not alarmed when, five weeks later, a regiment of government soldiers marched into their village under the pretense of seeking shelter and hospitality. The regiment of government soldiers was indeed mostly made up of Campbells, hostile opponents to the MacDonalds in a struggle that went back to the lost power of clan Donald and the Lord of the Isles and the steady rise to power of the Campbells over the years.

After 11 days sharing their dwellings and food and socializing with the MacDonalds, the soldiers rose at 5am one morning and carried out orders written up by John Dalrymple, The Master Of Stair, to put all to the sword under seventy the MacDonalds of Glencoe. The orders read:

> you are hereby ordered to fall upon the rabelle, the MacDonalds of Glencoe, and to putt all to the sword under seventy. You are to have a special care that the old fox and his sones doe not escape your hands. You are to secure all the avenues, that no man escape.

In all 33 men, 2 women and 2 children were executed while many perished trying to escape into the hills in the mid-winter cold and blizzards. At the old chief's house soldiers had been admitted asking to see the old man on a pressing matter. He was shot in the back of the head while putting on his trews and calling for refreshments.

This was regarded as the most shameful act of betrayal in Scottish history especially since Highland hospitality was held sacred, even among enemies. To this day there still exists an uneasiness between the Campbells and MacDonalds akin to that of the Highlands and the Lowlands or the Southern states towards the Northern states, at times in friendly rivalry and at times not so friendly. The Highlands would never be the same and their distrust for the government and the Lowlands would make it a logical place for a Jacobite uprising although when it did come they were still somewhat reluctant.

Culloden

With the death of Anne in 1714 and the accession of German George I, the wee German lairdie, hopes ran high that the House of Stuart could be restored. Plans were made over the next few years but attempts made in 1715 and 1719 failed miserably. A quarter of a century later few men could remember what life was like under a Stuart king and when Prince Charles Edward Stuart, the grandson of the deposed James VII and II, came to claim the throne for his father he was told to go home by the Highland chiefs. Nevertheless he did manage to raise a Highland Jacobite army against the government forces, of which a large part were Lowland Scots. The term Jacobite comes from the Latin Jacobus, for James, referring to James VII and II. Jacobites were the supporters of King James. Prince Charles' campaign ended in disaster with his defeat at the Battle of Culloden on April 16, 1746, the last pitched battle to be fought on British soil. Charles eventually escaped back to France, then to Italy, the country of his birth, where he died in Rome in 1788. There was a suggestion that after the colonies won their independence from Britain, Prince Charles should be offered the kingship of the new country but the Prince never considered it a serious offer and it really did not have much support in the former colonies. Although just a small number of the Highland clans took part in that final battle at Culloden, the results were felt by all. The aftermath of Culloden was to be cultural genocide at its worst. The wounded were slain on the field after the battle and Highlanders for months were rounded up and either executed or exiled. By an act of proscription, which stated in part "That from and after 1st of August 1747 no man or boy…shall on any pretense whatever, wear or put on the cloaths commonly called highland cloaths…", the Gaelic language was now outlawed as was the wearing of Highland dress. No Highlander was allowed to carry arms. The people were victimized, bullied and harassed. They were made to swear an oath in Gaelic on the holy iron of their dirks:

> "I do swear, as I shall answer to God at the great day of Judgment, I have not, nor shall I have in my possession any gun, sword, pistol or arm whatsoever, and never use tartan, plaid, or any part of the Highland Garb; and if I do so may I be cursed in my undertakings, family and property, may I be killed in battle as a coward, and lie without burial in a strange land, far from the graves of my forefathers and kindred; may all this come across me if I break my oath."

These laws were eventually repealed, but not until 1782.

By an Act of Parliament the clan chief had been stripped of his power over his clansmen and the only time Highlanders were allowed to wear Highland garb or carry weapons was when Highland regiments were formed to fight Britain's foreign wars. The Highlands were now being systematically stripped of its fighting men. The pacification of the Highlands had now begun.

Many regiments were formed and many Highlanders found themselves leaving their homeland and fighting fellow Scots in the colonies during the American Revolution, and in other places where the British Empire was expanding. With the absence of so many of its young men, the Highlands were now ripe for its next round of misfortunes.

The Highland Clearances

In 1792, a year known as The Year of the Sheep, Bliadhna nan Caorach in Gaelic, clearing of the people began when Highland Chiefs leased their lands out to Lowland sheep farmers. After 1745, being stripped of their power as warlords, they began to realize they were landlords. John Prebble explains it well in his book *Culloden*:

> Once the Chiefs lost their powers many of them lost also any parental interest in their clans men. During the next hundred years they continued the work of Cumberland's battalions. So that they might lease their glens and braes to sheep-farmers from the Lowlands and England, they cleared the crofts of men, women and children, using police and soldiers where necessary.

Said John MacLachlan of Rahoy, (1804-1870), a Gaelic speaking poet:

> Heavy, sorrowful my heart, going through the glen
> On an April morning I no longer hear
> birdsongs, or the lowing of cattle on the moor.
> I hear the unpleasant noise of sheep
> And the English language, and dogs barking
> And frightening the deer.

The Highland Clearances were to last from 1792 well into the 1800s, when in 1886 a Crofters' Holding Act bill was passed to meet the demands of the Highland Land Law Reform Association. Although emigration had started well before then, from 1745 onwards the Highlanders were being forced to leave their mountains and glens to find a new way of life in Canada, the colonies or the Lowlands. Between 1763 and 1775 20,000 people left for the colonies, some the families of soldiers who had been awarded tracts of land, others escaping dire conditions. Some left from Greenock, but the cost of sailing from a Scottish port such as Greenock, the most important port for departing emigrants, was more expensive than sailing from Ireland. Many crossed the Irish Sea to sail from Dublin or Belfast. Having sailed from Ireland, some of these emigrants were erroneously listed as Irish in their new destinations. The conditions of these emigrant ships were deplorable, with too many people crammed in and with not enough provisions for the journey. Due to the number of people who died on the crossings, they would be referred to as coffin ships by the Irish, who later experienced similar conditions leaving Ireland during the potato famines of the 1840s. In 1773 such a ship left for the Carolinas with four hundred and fifty passengers, each having about two square feet of deck for eleven weeks with sour water to drink. Before they reached their destination twenty-three had died of dysentery. Over the years many cases worse than that would be recorded.

Although life in the Lowlands was much easier than that of the Highlands, it was still well behind the standards of English dwellers. Poverty, religious and cultural differences and general lawlessness among other things gave good reason why an ambitious Lowland Scot should look elsewhere for a better life. Old hatreds ran deep between the Highlands and Lowlands. When emigration to new worlds began, especially to the American colonies, these hatreds often followed.

So now let's look at how the history of Scotland and England would affect America.

Scottish Influence in American History

"Every line of strength in American history is a line colored with Scottish blood"
- American President Woodrow Wilson.

Scottish Emigration

Whether we believe that America was discovered by Norse Vikings led by Leif Eriksson in the 11th century or perhaps early Celts following Brendan The Explorer, (born C. 484/486 died 578), the biggest influence in North America was felt after the arrival of Columbus. The nations claiming colonies in the new world included France, Spain and England. We do know that the Scots had a lot to do with the development of the original English colonies or British America, but they were just that, English colonies. Any attempts to establish Scottish colonies met with opposition from England. In 1695, in the face of English defiance and hostility, the Scots tried to form a colony of their own in Central America to make Scotland a great trading nation and to give some independence to its people and to free them from continuing famine and despair among others things. The colony formed in the isthmus of Panama became known as The Darien Disaster. The end of this Scottish endeavor came in 1698 and forced Scotland into the Union of the Governments in 1707, an event not welcomed by most of Scotland. Robert Burns would later write,

> We're bought and sold for English gold
> Such a parcel of rogues in a nation.

In all events it did give Scotland greater trading powers, they could now trade anywhere and what were once English colonies now became British. Prior to this, many Scots were already in the colonies, but the wave of immigration now picked up and Scottish Lowlanders poured into the Northeast. Highlanders, particularly after Culloden, came mainly to the Carolinas. Ulster Scots, those who were to be known later as Scotch-Irish, were also emigrating in great numbers.

Scotland has been a country of emigrants from the very early days due to harsh conditions in a poor land. When Samuel Johnson, English poet, essayist, critic and journalist, and his Scottish companion, James Boswell, visited the Isle of Skye in 1773 they found what they called "an epidemical fury of emigration. "The islanders even had a dance reel they called "America" in which the broad circular movements showed "how emigration catches till all are set afloat."

During the 1700s and 1800s London encouraged only one Scottish industry: the export of its people. When soldiers were needed, the British Empire found whole regiments from the Highlands. When the British Empire expanded, Scotsmen played key roles in its administration. In the East India Company, more than a quarter of the army's officers were Scotsmen and many of the civilian officers in Madras and Bengal were also Scots. For centuries Scottish mercenaries have fought in many countries for many different causes.

Scotch

I would like to add a little on the word Scotch as many these days insist it should only be used when referring to Scotch whisky. The word Scotch dates only from the end of the 16th century, but was the predominant adjective in the 18th and 19th centuries. It is a contraction of Scottish and ousted Scottish as the prevailing form in England in the 18th-century and later in Scotland itself.

Going back to 700 AD when the Anglo-Saxons were settled in Lowland Scotland up to the 16th and 17th centuries, to the time of Mary Queen of Scots and James the VI and I, the language of Scotland was referred to as Northern English. It was the official language of the Scottish kingdom, a kingdom rich in literature. If Scotland had remained an independent kingdom it would have probably become a separate language known eventually as Lallans with several different dialects. King James' VI native tongue was Lallans although he was quite proficient in Latin and French and when he had to he could also speak in southern lowland English, but with a strong Scottish accent. Mary Queen of Scots spoke Lallans better than she could English.

The union of the crowns in 1603 began a long process of assimilation. Gradually, the more populous and wealthier southern partner would impose its standard language on the Scottish nation. To the English it was only natural that the English language and culture would be adopted unquestionably as the sole medium of official communication in the United Kingdom but even at the time of the union of the governments in 1707 standard English was relatively limited. Dr. Johnson's *A Dictionary of the English Language* (1755) states in the preface that the English language is "copious without order, energetic without rules", and he tamed both vocabulary and grammar. In referring to the language his goal was elimination. "Scotch is not much heard except now and then by an old lady", he said. During the 18th century, under pressure of enlightenment, standardization was thought to be beneficial. The process of assimilation was stepped up not just for the elimination of Gaelic and Lallans but including regional dialects of the English and the Welsh. Lallans was in firm use though and even the word Scotch was much preferred to Scottish or Scots but under an increasingly anglicized society it was becoming the language of the poor and uncouth. Burns apparently thought English was the proper medium for serious thought but wrote his worst poems in it. His best works were written in the language of the peasant society who inspired him and of which he was a member. Other writers of his time and later would not completely abandon the "auld scotch tongue" but would use it to write both song and story. The Scotch word remained prevalent in the works of Scott, Stevenson and Barrie. In fact, Barrie objected to what he called the newfangled word "Scots". So it was that in the Plantation of Ulster from 1610 onwards, when James colonized Northern Ireland with mostly Lowland Scottish farmers, they took with them their culture, religion and language including the good auld Scotch word. The Scotch-Irish, along with Scottish emigrants, took it to America and Canada. Canadian writer, economist, teacher and politician John Kenneth Galbraith wrote a book entitled the "The Scotch" published in 1964 not about whisky but about the people. It is a history of the Scotch in Canada in which he states "they were never called Scots." Scottish writer Clifford

Hanley wrote "A Skinful of Scotch" in 1965 which was about Scotland and its people, not a boozer's guide to Bonnie Scotland. Clifford Hanley is also the writer of the words to "Scotland The Brave" one of Scotland's unofficial national anthems.

The Scotch-Irish

It was James VI of Scotland, who reigned from 1603 to 1625, who began the colonization of Northern Ireland with mostly Scottish Lowland farmers. These people were among the poorest and most backward of all in the European countries, but they took with them a passion for education and a vision for a better way of life. They were given long leases in Northern Ireland, common terms being for a period of 21 years. King James had specifically excluded Highlanders for his Plantation of Ulster, for their Gaelic tongue and Catholicism made them more welcome to the native Irish and it was James' wish to civilize Ireland by making them more British. Therefore in the history and the ancestry of the Scotch-Irish there was no place for the Highlanders. Those Lowland Scots who took the challenge became the ancestors of all the Scotch-Irish in America. By 1700 the plantation was a success and Ulster was far and above the rest of Ireland in many ways. It was experiencing economic prosperity and a high standard of education but was now a threat to the English economy. Trade laws were changed to protect England which eventually made it difficult for Ulster to continue to prosper in the way it had. Consequently, unhappy Ulster Scots turned to the New World for a brighter future, rather than continue its ongoing fight with English ways and laws. When leases ran out, the highest bidder for new leases was usually native Irishmen, so the Ulster Scot had a choice of either Scotland or the New World. The Irish, on the other hand, saw the opportunity to gain back the hold on their own land, and had no desire to leave Ireland. The Irish themselves did not migrate to America in great numbers until they were forced to do so during the 1840s as a result of the great potato famines. This later wave would be Irish Catholics as opposed to the protestant Ulster Scots who would arrive before them. In his book *Three Roads to the Alamo* William C. Davies states, "Despite the misnomer 'Scotch-Irish,' they were almost all Scots, a story of a whole population of the poor who started moving from the British Isles in the 1700s and never stopped." The majority of the Scotch-Irish who came to the American colonies settled in Pennsylvania, Virginia and the Carolinas; however, there were many others in all of the thirteen colonies. Highland and Lowland Scots also settled throughout Nova Scotia and New Jersey. The descendants of those Scotch-Irish who originally went to Pennsylvania, Virginia and the Carolinas went on to Georgia, Kentucky and Tennessee in the 1780s and 1790s. At the same time, the Scotch-Irish who landed in Philadelphia made their way down the Appalachian valleys into Virginia and beyond. They came for many reasons, but high rents and religious persecution were perhaps the most prevalent.

These Scots and Scotch-Irish came in later than the English and European settlers but their culture and influence have been strongly felt throughout American history, especially in the South where most of them settled. Since the Scots were often educated, planters in the Chesapeake region often hired them as tutors, but were upset when their children began speaking with a Scottish brogue. In Celeste Ray's book, *Highland Heritage, Scottish Americans in the American South*, she identifies the different waves of Scottish immigrants. The Scotch-Irish, the Highland Scots, and the Lowland Scots all came over during different time periods, but all influenced early Southern history in many ways. Some Southern communities spoke nothing but Gaelic and others spoke with very heavy Scottish brogues.

Lowland Scots and Scotch-Irish played an important part in American colonial life, especially in the Piedmont areas of Virginia and the Carolinas. Scottish merchants were found in all major cities and also played an important part in overseas trade. In the Southern colonies they were prominent in official capacities, serving as governors, clerks, clergymen and educators. Eventually, Scottish explorers, administrators, diplomats, adventurers, bankers, merchants, soldiers, sailors, engineers, missionaries and doctors made their mark not only on the colonies but the entire New World.

The first U.S. census, taken in 1790, showed the Celtic descendants outnumbered the Anglo-Saxons by two to one in the South. Approximately three-fourths of the Caucasian race in the South before the Civil War was of Celtic (mostly Scottish) descendants. The Scottish influence was so prominent in the South during the Civil War that it is thought that the blood-curdling rebel yell came from the battle cry of the Highlanders. As late as 1851 the "Raleigh Register" reported that many in the area still spoke Gaelic.

Georgia was also a popular destination of the Scottish emigrants. James Oglethorpe, founder of Georgia, in 1732 invited many to settle along the southern frontier, and help defend it. The colony grew rapidly around the town of Savannah, and by early 1736 there were some 2000 colonists, including the southernmost town called Darien, established that year by Scottish Highlanders. One incentive he used was to allow the Scots to keep their dress, customs, language and tradition, since use of Highland dress had been banned in Scotland by the British government. Oglethorpe was even known to wear the Highland dress when visiting the settlements. Throughout colonial America, the Scots were prominent in the areas of business, medical science, philosophic thought, academic excellence, and teaching.

The Scottish influence in the development of the new nation was huge. Historians have explored in detail the numerous theological, political, economic, medical, educational, and evangelical influences that Scotland had in Colonial America. If one includes folkways, culture, and music in the list, it could be argued that the Scots and Scotch-Irish had more influence in molding early American institutions and lifestyles than any other European group.

The Scots and the American Revolutionary Way

When the Revolutionary War broke out, the Scotch-Irish, especially those who had come from Scotland to Ireland to America, were eager to fight the British Crown. One Hessian officer is reported to have said, "Call this war by whatever name you may---it is nothing more or less than a Scotch-

Irish Presbyterian rebellion." King George is said to have called the conflict "a Presbyterian war", a reference to the official Church of Scotland.

However, apart from the Scotch-Irish, many Scottish Highlanders were coming to the colonies after the Battle of Culloden and were actually more divided in their loyalties. Many of them sided with Great Britain when the American Revolutionary war broke out. Many Scots who settled in the New World were fiercely loyal to the Crown because of their strong ties to clan and country. Scotland remained in their hearts, and because Scotland was part of the United Kingdom they remained loyal. After the war, approximately 30,000 loyal Scots left for Canada, including "the reluctant heroine", Flora MacDonald, and her husband Allan. Flora was the young Highland lass who helped Bonnie Prince Charlie escape the clutches of the government forces in 1746 when, after Culloden, he was fleeing through the Highlands with a price of £30,000 on his head. After a short imprisonment in the Tower of London for her part in the Prince's escape, Flora was released and returned to Skye where she married Allan MacDonald of Kingsburgh, Skye, and they emigrated to the Carolinas in 1751. Allan was fighting for the government forces of King George when he was captured and Flora fled to Nova Scotia. In 1779, Flora returned to South Uist and lived with her brother until Allan's release. He joined her once again in Kingsburgh where she eventually died in 1790. Of the 23,000 who immigrated to the colonies between 1764 and 1776 after the Battle of Culloden, most settled with their fellow clansmen and retained the ways of clan life. Today, many historians feel that more descendants of the Highland clans are in North America than in Scotland.

However, I feel that one way or another the Scots in general brought the seed of freedom and independence to the colonies, and it was just a matter of time before it took root and grew.

Col. John Henry was born in Scotland and about 1773 married Sarah Winston Syme, whose father was Welsh. Their son, Patrick Henry, is famous for the line "Give me liberty or give me death". Although such sentiments were not uncommon in the colonies against the crown and

Britain he was accused of treason when giving the speech that contained that line. He is often illustrated as being under-educated but nevertheless rose to prominence as a great orator and American statesmen. It reminds me somewhat of Robert Burns who has been generally regarded as an unlettered peasant with a touch of poetic inspiration, yet when he arrived in Edinburgh, the titled and literary authorities were quite taken aback at the extent, variety and range of his knowledge and acquirements. Both men were influenced by their fathers to a great extent, and although not much formal education is in their upbringing, both certainly had a great thirst for reading and history. Patrick Henry's father was a well-educated Scotsman who taught him Latin, Greek and mathematics for five years. Henry read and reread histories of Greece, Rome and England, and if one reads the history of England, one reads the history of Scotland. Judging by the ancestry of Robert Burns' parents, William Burnes and Agnes Brown, although peasants themselves, they were peasants well equipped for the rearing of good men and women. Children born to them were intellectually superior to the average class of peasant that they were part of. Both Burns and Henry were radicals and like Henry, Burns was accused of treason for his sympathy towards the British Reform movement, an idea born of the French Revolution. By having some friends in the right places he avoided being sent to Botany Bay. Burns had ideas of emigrating to the colonies at some point and had he done so what a meeting of minds between Henry and Burns there could have been.

Famous Scottish Americans

The Scots played an important part in the founding of this country and in securing American freedom. One of the most prominent historical figures is Sam Wilson, known as "Uncle Sam". Uncle Sam's parents emigrated from Greenock, Scotland. Uncle Sam's father was one of the Minute Men in the early stages of the American Revolution. Sam became a butcher and meat packager near Albany, New York and supplied meat to the U.S. army in years after the war of independence and apparently during the war of 1812. As the story goes, a meat inspector visited Sam's plant one day and asked for the boss. An Irish employee replied that he would be looking for Uncle Sam, a name that would be personified to mean the

United States, the initials being the same. Later, recruiting posters for the army stated "I Want You For U.S. Army" with a painting of what was supposed to be the original Uncle Sam, but the artist actually used his own image. The western seaport of Greenock, Scotland, was one of the busiest ports in Scotland, especially for emigration to North America. Although Sam Wilson's parents emigrated from this port, there is no certainty that they were native Greenockians. It has also been believed that Scottish-born Captain Kidd, privateer out of New York in the late 1600s, was born in Greenock. More recent evidence has him hailing from Dundee. He most likely sailed from Greenock, hence the mix up.

Several signers of the Declaration of Independence were Scotch-Irish, and two were Scottish-born: Reverend John Witherspoon, and James Wilson. John Witherspoon was the only ordained clergyman to sign. In 1768, he came to the American colonies from Scotland to take the post of president of the College of New Jersey (Princeton University). While in Scotland he was the leader of the evangelical party in the Kirk, but also followed the Common Sense philosophies. He included many of the ideas of the Scottish Enlightenment in Princeton's curriculum.

The other Scottish signer of the Declaration was James Wilson, who was educated at St. Andrews, Edinburgh and Glasgow but never graduated. At 23, he came to the colonies and tutored at the College of Philadelphia where he received an honorary degree of Master of Arts. He later was admitted to the Philadelphia bar in 1767. In 1774, he wrote a legal opinion that stated that unless Americans had representation in the British parliament, the parliament had no authority to legislate over them. This later became the grounds that caused the break with Britain - taxation without representation. The following year, 1775, Wilson made a speech which said that Parliament was possibly unconstitutional for passing laws not intended by England's constitution. This formed the basis of Judicial Review, the American system in which acts passed by government can be checked against the constitution. This later became the Supreme Court. The name Wilson figured prominently in American history. There were at least six Wilsons in the Texas army, two of whom died at the Alamo, 32-

year-old John Wilson from Pennsylvania and 29-year-old David L. Wilson from Scotland.

John Paul Jones, America's first naval hero and founder of the U.S. Navy, was born in Kirkcudbright, Scotland. He developed the concept of a naval academy in which naval life was taught by navy people, as opposed to inexperienced bureaucrats. His remains now lie at the Naval Academy in Annapolis, MD, under a 24-hour guard.

Other famous Americans with Scottish ties are: Andrew Carnegie, wealthy industrialist and philanthropist; Allan Pinkerton, founder of the Pinkerton Detective Agency, who provided protection for President Lincoln and monitoring of Confederate troops during the Civil War; John Muir, founder of the National Parks system; and James Wilson, Secretary of Agriculture who revolutionized America's approach to agriculture, research, soil conservation, reforestation, plant disease, insect control, weather forecasting, inspection of food, and improvements of rural roads.

Of the governors of the original thirteen states, nine were Scots. The first Secretary of War, Gen. Henry Knox, was Scottish, as was the first Surgeon-General, James Craik. The great orator during the Revolutionary period, Patrick Henry, had a Scottish father, as did Alexander Hamilton, whose contributions to the Federalist Essays helped formulate ideas found in the U.S. Constitution. Hamilton also served as the First Secretary of the U.S. Treasury.

Another important colonial American with great influence was Thomas Jefferson, author of the Declaration of Independence. Jefferson was of Scottish and Welsh lineage, a descendant of Randolphs and Keiths. He also came under the influence of two prominent Scots during his college years at William and Mary. William Small, a mathematics and natural philosophy professor, has been noted as a major source of inspiration to Jefferson. Jefferson once referred to him as being like a father to him. "Small...would not have been a true Scot if he had not had the passionate love for discussion and logic which seems the innate gift of so many sons of the Highlands," wrote historian Gilbert Chinard in *Thomas Jefferson:*

The Apostle of Americanism. Also while at William and Mary, Jefferson was exposed to the writings of the Scottish Lord Henry Home Kames. "Here he found a definition of society which he could have written himself and which expresses his political individualism and subordination to law," according to Chinard. It was the time of Enlightenment that influenced Jefferson and this thought could possibly go as far back as April 6, 1320 and the writing of the Declaration of Arbroath.

Other important Scottish-Americans were: Donald MacKay, naval architect and builder of clipper ships; Andrew Jackson, Stonewall Jackson, Jeb Stuart, Andrew Carnegie, Alexander Graham Bell, General Patton, General Douglas MacArthur, John William MacKay, discoverer of the Comstock Lode and organizer of the Commercial Cable Company; and his son Clarence Hungerford Mackay, supervisor of the construction of the first trans-Pacific cable between the U.S. and the Far East in 1904. The first man to set foot on the moon, Neil Armstrong, was of Scottish ancestry and the first sport to be played on the moon was the Scottish game of golf.

Scottish Influence Found in American Documents

It has been said that the American Declaration of Independence was influenced by the Declaration of Arbroath. The Declaration of Arbroath was prepared as a formal Declaration of Independence of Scotland. It was drawn up in Arbroath Abbey on the 6th of April 1320, most likely by the Abbot, Bernard de Linton, who was also the Chancellor of Scotland. The Declaration urged the Pope to see things from a Scottish perspective and not to take the English claim on Scotland seriously. It said in part:

> But from these countless evils we have been set free, by the help of Him Who though he afflicts yet heals and restores, by our most tireless Prince, King and Lord, the Lord Robert. He, that his people and his heritage might be delivered out of the hands of our enemies, met toil and fatigue, hunger and peril, like another Macabaeus or Joshua and bore them cheerfully. Him, too, divine providence, his right of succession according to our

laws and customs which we shall maintain to the death, and the due consent and assent of us all have made our Prince and King. To him, as to the man by whom salvation has been wrought unto our people, we are bound both by law and by his merits that our freedom may be still maintained, and by him, come what may, we mean to stand.

Yet, if he should give up what he has begun, and agree to make us or our kingdom subject to the King of England or the English, we should exert ourselves at once to drive him out as our enemy and a subverter of his own rights and ours, and make some other man who was well able to defend us our King; for, as long as but a hundred of us remain alive, never will we on any conditions be brought under English rule. It is in truth not for glory, nor riches, nor honours that we are fighting, but for freedom-for that alone, which no honest man gives up but with life itself.

Earlier and later American documents contained the same philosophies. An example is the Virginia Declaration of Rights, written by George Mason and adopted by the Virginia Constitutional Convention on June 12, 1776:

> Section 3. That government is, or ought to be, instituted for the common benefit protection and security of the people, nation, or community; of all the various modes and forms of government, that is best which is capable of producing the greatest degree of happiness and safety and is most effectual secured against the danger of maladministration. And that, when any government shall be found inadequate or contrary to these purposes, a majority of the community has an indubitable, inalienable, and indefeasible right to reform, alter or abolish it, in such a manner as shall be judged most conducive to the public weal.

When the Continental Congress gave Thomas Jefferson the task of drafting a Declaration of Independence he drew upon the Virginia

Declaration of Rights when writing the opening paragraphs. Similarly, the American Declaration of Independence states:

> "That whenever any Form of Government becomes destructive of these ends, it is the Right of the People to alter or abolish it, and to institute new Government, laying its foundation on such principles and organizing its powers in such form, as to them shall seem most likely to effect their Safety and Happiness...When a long train of abuses and usurpations, pursuing invariably the same Object evinces a design to reduce them under absolute despotism, it is their right, it is their duty, to throw off such a government and provide new Guards for their future security."

Interestingly although the Virginia declaration was adopted by the Virginia Constitutional Convention on June 12th, 1776, another declaration of independence had been drawn up by the Scotch-Irish of Mecklenburg County in North Carolina dated May 20th, 1775. From that day they were no longer subject to British rule. It gives North Carolinians the boast of being "First for Freedom". In 1817 William Wirt's publication "Life of Patrick Henry" putting forth the claim that "Mr. Henry certainly gave the first impulse to the ball of the Revolution," sparked a resentment between Massachusetts and Virginia over who played the most important roll in the initial struggle. Unfortunately the original documents and written records from the Mecklenburg Meetings were destroyed by a fire on, of all dates, April 6th, 1800. The secretary of the committee, John McNitt Alexander, in whose house the fire took place, transcribed two copies from memory on September 3rd of that year, one of which ended up in the hands of his friend General William R. Davie. This copy became known as the "Davie Copy". A copy was sent to Thomas Jefferson from John Adams who stated that he thought the declaration to be genuine and "The genuine sense of America at that moment was never expressed so well before or since". This Jefferson took exception to as it also brought up a question of possible plagiarism. In reply to John Adams he thought the Mecklenburg document to be spurious. Webster's dictionary defines spurious as 1. Illegitimate; bastard. 2. Counterfeit; not genuine. The fact is that throughout the colonies this seed of independence had been brought with the various migrations of Scotch-Irish, Lowland and Highland Scots, most with a very intimate knowledge of their history, that it would not be uncommon they would go to that source for inspiration, The Declaration of Arbroath.

On March 2, 1836, when Texas drew up its own Declaration of Independence, it is obvious that the U.S. Declaration of Independence served as a model. The Texas Declaration of Independence states:

> "When a government has ceased to protect the life, liberty and property of the people, from whom its legitimate powers are derived, and for the advancement of whose happiness it was instituted, and so far from being a guarantee for the enjoyment of these inestimable and inalienable rights becomes an instrument in the hands of evil rulers for their oppression....When in consequence of such acts of malfeasance and abdication on the part of the government, anarchy prevails, and civil society is dissolved into its original elements. In such a crisis, the first law of nature, the right of self-preservation, inherent and inalienable rights of the people to appeal to first principles, and take their political affairs into their own hands in extreme cases, enjoins it as a right towards themselves and a sacred obligation to their posterity, to abolish such government and create another in its stead..."

Thus, we see the influence of the Scottish Declaration of Arbroath (April 6, 1320) as it evolved through the Virginia Declaration of Rights, the U.S. Declaration of Independence and the Texas Declaration of Independence. It came up once more shortly after the Mexican war when a freshman Whig Congressman opposed to Mr. Polk's War as unconstitutional, stated "Any people anywhere, being inclined and having the power have the right to rise up and shake off the existing government, and form a new one that suits them better... any portion of such people that can may revolutionize and make their own of the territory as they inhabit"

A decade later the actions of that congressman would contradict the words he'd spoken. The congressman was Abraham Lincoln.

Nowhere is there a better comparison of the Declaration of Independence and the Arbroath Declaration than in *The Mark of the Scots* written by Duncan A. Bruce. It is breakdown that leaves little doubt of the origin of the American document.

The Declaration of Arbroath has become such an important historical event for Scotland and freedom lovers around the world that it is observed each year as a time to celebrate Scottish roots. Numerous groups and societies throughout Canada and America have taken the anniversary of the Declaration of Arbroath (April 6, 1320) as their national date to celebrate their Scottish roots. On December 19th 1991, in response to action initiated by the Clans & Scottish Societies of Canada, the Ontario Legislature passed a resolution proclaiming April 6th as Tartan Day, following the example of other Canadian provinces. America followed suit on March 20th 1998, when Senate Resolution 155 (S. Res. 155), proposed by U.S. Senate Republican majority leader Trent Lott, was passed unanimously proclaiming April 6 Tartan Day.

Scotland, The Alamo, and Texas

Scottish Influences in Texas History

Many of the leaders at the Alamo were of Scottish descent and the Scottish culture was a major influence in their actions both on and off the battlefield. A majority of those who went to Texas to tame the rugged frontier and establish a republic were of Scottish or Celtic descent. Four Scots died at the Alamo and 80% of the others were of Scotch-Irish descent. Of the 189 men who died defending the Alamo, there was one Welshman, thirteen Irishmen, and fifteen Englishmen.

More than eighty-five percent of the pioneers who followed Stephen F. Austin into the Mexican state of Coahuila y Tejas were of Celtic origin, and half of those were Scottish. Moses Austin, of the clan Keith, initially dreamed of taking a group of Americans into the Spanish Territory of Tejas. On January 27, 1821 a petition was granted to Moses Austin to bring a small band of American colonists into Texas to create a buffer between the Spanish settlements and the Indians. However, Moses Austin died before his dream could be fulfilled and his son, Stephen F. Austin took up his father's cause.

To make a smooth transition and to avoid problems, Austin chose only those from the "better" classes. In all, 307 titles were granted to 297 grantees and of those, only four could not read. A majority of grantees were of Scottish descent; two names were German, eight French, and two Dutch. The remainder had last names that were affiliated to Scottish clans or Celtic stock from the British Isles.

The most prized possession of that time was land, something that had been denied to their ancestors in Scotland and Ireland. The new Texans were willing to work hard and face isolation and Indians in order to hold on to the land. The ultimate test of this resolve was found at the Alamo.

I have tried at this point to stay close to the history of Scotland and to pinpoint the influence of the Scots and their ancestors in the colonies/states/Southern states and Texas, so that when we eventually get to the Alamo music, with the bagpipes and fiddle music and songs they sang, we will better understand who these people were. I will now look at some of the individuals involved and their backgrounds, but I could not resist touching on some of the most intriguing aspects of the Alamo, whether they be Scottish or not. We will never get a clear picture of the absolute truth of it all. Did Crockett wear a coonskin cap? Did he die fighting or was he executed? Did Travis draw a line in the sand? How many actually died? The list of truly unanswerable questions is long, but I would like to add my observations on some of them. We also need to look at some Texas and Alamo history.

A Brief History of The Alamo

Mission San Antonio de Valero, the first mission in San Antonio, was established on May 1st, 1718, on the west bank of the San Antonio River, by Franciscan Father Olivares. It was named in honor of the Marquis of Valero, viceroy of Mexico. On May 5th, four days later, a village and a fort were founded, both named in honor of the Duke of Bexar, a Spanish hero and the viceroy's brother. The village was named Villa de Bexar and the fort was named Presidio de San Antonio de Bexar. The fort was built for the protection of the village and the mission from Indians. The mission was moved shortly after to the richer lands of the east bank, but was destroyed by a hurricane in 1724. It was moved to its present location thereafter. The first church of the mission was started in 1744. Built of stone, it collapsed in 1756, and two years later the present church was built. In 1793, the mission was no longer used by the Church and most of the property was turned over to the Indians who continued to live there.

When the Spanish arrived in the late 1680s, the area around the San Antonio River valley was occupied by Payaya Indians, but with the founding of the mission and the fort, others settlers were finding their way there. In 1731, Spain brought in settlers from the Canary Islands, a Spanish province off the west coast of Africa. In all, 56 people making up

16 families arrived and set up what was to be the first civil settlement in Texas with an elected alcalde (mayor) and cabildo (council). They laid out plans for the village, which included a plaza and a church. The church would later be called the San Fernando Cathedral.

Alamo means "cottonwood" in Spanish. However, the name originates from a Spanish cavalry troop from Alamo de Parras in Mexico. They occupied the abandoned mission from about a decade after it was discontinued as a mission until 1821, when it was taken over by Mexican troops at the conclusion of the Mexican Revolution. It became known as "Pueblo del Alamo". Mexico had gained its independence from Spain with a revolution that lasted from 1813 to 1821.

The Settlement of Texas

Additional settlement of the San Antonio area began in 1821, when the Mexican authorities opened the province of Texas to foreign settlement, realizing the need to occupy the vast area of Texas. The Mexican authorities gave the settlers tax and customs abatements but did not include government services such as defense. The new settlements governed themselves and soon the newcomers (Texians or Texans) outnumbered the original Mexican population (Tejanos) by 5 to 1. The terms, Texians or Texans referred to newcomers to Texas, mostly from the Southern states, and Tejanos were Mexicans born in Texas. In 1823, Mexico passed the Imperial Colonization Law, the first of several, encouraging settlers to the Texas area. In 1824, the new Mexican government redefined territories as states joining two separate territories into one state, Tejas y Coahuila, and moved the capital from San Antonio to Saltillo, 365 miles away and allowed representatives (two from Texas and eleven from Coahuila) in the state government. This turned out to be an unpopular move with the settlers and armed protests were staged. Colonization was halted in 1830 when a law was passed on April 6th of that year. The unrest had culminated in 1832 with the taking of a Mexican fort on Galveston Bay by the Texans.

In 1833, Stephen F. Austin, representing the settlers, traveled to Mexico City to try to persuade the then new president Santa Anna to recognize Texas and Coahuila as separate states. The political unrest ended when Santa Anna rose to power and revoked the Mexican Constitution of 1824. He also dissolved local legislatures and imposed central control. The Texans soon discovered that their political conventions were considered acts of treason. The Mexican government was losing control and tried to take it back, but many troubles were brewing. Many factors aggravated the situation:

- Many Mexicans suspected that the settlers represented a covert U.S. effort to seize Texas. As an example they pointed to the fact that in Florida, Spain ceded control to the U.S. after an American general occupied it during "hot pursuit" of Indians across the border. That general was now president of the United States - Andrew Jackson.
- Mutual ethnic prejudice.
- Many of the American settlers ("Texians") were Southerners who believed in and practiced slavery.

Tension continued with skirmishes occurring periodically. On December 10, 1835, a Mexican garrison of 1,105 surrendered and evacuated the Alamo, and the Texans took over. On January 3, 1836, the Texan government authorized a raid on Matamoras, Mexico, but failed to establish a clear chain of command. They eventually named four different commanders including Sam Houston, and Col. James Fannin, a West Point attendee who had resigned after two years in the academy. Many of those who gathered to fight were American adventurers rather than Texan settlers who had gone home for the spring planting. On January 10, 1836, many from the Texan ruling council complained that the Alamo had been stripped of cannons and supplies for the Matamoras expedition. On January 17, 1836, Sam Houston sent Jim Bowie and about 20 men to the Alamo with orders to destroy it. On January 20, 1836, William B. Travis arrived at the Alamo with 30 men he had recruited for the Texan "regular army." On February 8, 1836, former Tennessee congressman David "Davy" Crockett arrived with about a dozen of his "Tennessee volunteers". On February 11, 1836, Col. James Neill, official commander of the Alamo, left for personal business, leaving Travis in command. The garrison, however, held an election and elected Bowie. The two agreed to be co-commanders.

February 15, 1836: Santa Anna arrived at the Rio Grande, near present-day Eagle Pass. He commanded that every Texan rebel be executed or exiled, the other settlers sent to the interior and replaced with Mexican settlers, and immigration stopped.

February 16, 1836: Fannin at Goliad got the first of several appeals for aid from Travis at the Alamo. Fannin refused.

February 23, 1836: the siege of the Alamo began. The defenders were outnumbered ten to one but are the only things standing in the way of the destruction of Texas. They had an assortment of nearly two dozen cannon but a shortage of technical skills and equipment made them nearly unusable.

February 24, 1836: Travis sent out his famous appeal for reinforcements.

February 27, 1836: Travis sent out another appeal to Fannin carried by his close friend and fellow South Carolinian, James Butler Bonham. When Bonham began his journey back to the Alamo another rider begged him not to return to certain death. He did return and reported the negative results of his mission.

March 2, 1836: a new Texas government declared independence from Mexico.

March 4, 1836: Fannin finally decided to head toward the Alamo, but only four miles into the journey wagons began breaking down and he turned back. That night a woman left the Alamo and reported to Santa Anna that the defenses were crumbling and about to collapse. She urged him to attack immediately.

March 6, 1836: the Alamo was stormed before dawn. The Mexicans were not able to scale the wall until the third attempt. The size of the initial attack force was approximately 1400 to about 189 defenders. Most sources agree that the attack lasted about 1½ hours. When the attack ended, the Alamo was destroyed and approximately 189 Texans and 1600 Mexicans lay dead.

March 11, 1836: Sam Houston reached Gonzales. He heard of the fate of the Alamo and ordered Fannin to join him but Fannin did not respond in a timely fashion. Fannin went to Goliad and as he was moving his troops out of Goliad he was soon surrounded and pinned down.

March 20, 1836: Fannin surrendered unconditionally and has the understanding that he and his men will be expelled from Mexico.

March 27, 1836: Fannin and his men are marched out of Goliad under Santa Anna's orders and shot.

March 28, 1836: the Mexican army advanced from San Antonio and began burning Texan settlements. Houston was at the Brazos River with approximately 1400 troops.

April 1836: most Texans abandoned their land and fled to the Louisiana border that was also the U.S. border.

April 18, 1836: Houston's scout, Deaf Smith, captured a Mexican courier. His papers showed the planned Mexican movements. The courier's saddlebags carried the monogram "W.B. Travis".

April 21, 1836: Houston's force of 918 overran Santa Anna's troops of 1200 while they were taking a siesta.

April 22, 1836: Santa Anna was found hiding in the bushes and captured. He agreed to recognize Texas' independence and ordered all Mexican forces to evacuate Texas. The war for Texas independence was won at the

Battle of San Jacinto with the Texans crying, "Remember the Alamo!" and "Remember Goliad!"

After the Battle of San Jacinto, Texas became an independent republic. At the end of 1845, Texas was annexed by the United States at its request. The annexation led to the war with Mexico and the expansion of the continental U.S. to nearly its present borders.

Key Figures In Early Texas History

Sam Houston

Fight on, brave knights! Man dies, but glory lives! Fight on, brave knights! Death is better than defeat! Fight on, brave knights, for bright eyes behold your deeds!
  - Sir Walter Scott, *Ivanhoe*

The Houston ancestry can be traced back to archers who led the way for Joan of Arc, from Orleans to Reims, to the Norman invasion of England in 1066, and to Sir Hugh of Padivan, a Norman knight and retainer of William the Conqueror. In the thick of battle, Sir Hugh saved the life of Malcolm III Canmore of Scotland, who reigned from 1057-1093. For this, he was awarded an addition to his coat-of-arms of two swift greyhounds supporting the motto "IN TEMPORE" over his older Norman coat-of-arms of three ravens. They would become part of the minor nobility of Scotland. Sam's great-great-grandfather, Sir John Houston, built the family's baronial estate near Johnstone, Scotland. A town now exists which still bears the family name. John Houston, Sam's great-grandfather, sought refuge in Northern Ireland in protest against religious and political persecution, he being an adherent of John Knox. Although his roots were deep in Scotland, he abandoned hope of returning there and in 1735 turned toward the New World with his wife Margaret, six children and an aging mother.

He lived in Pennsylvania with his family, where he prospered fairly well, but with the German population increasing in that area and the prospect of better opportunities, he followed the stream of Scotch-Irish Presbyterians into Virginia. John acquired land in Virginia, near Lexington and was able to add acres to this land from time to time. His plantation was called Timber Ridge, and after his death resulting from a falling tree limb in 1754 at the age of sixty-five, it passed down through his sons to Samuel, Sam's father, as a productive and prosperous farm. Samuel was more interested in maintaining his military career and he disregarded the management of the plantation, which was sold off bit by bit. Sam Houston's mother, Elizabeth (nee Paxton), was also Scottish. Her family, like her husband's, came from the Highlands to Virginia by way of Ireland.

Sam was born in Rockbridge County, Virginia, on March 2nd, 1793. He was not destined to be a farmer and bucked family tradition by leaving the farm and heading southwest until he came to a Cherokee Indian village run by Chief Oolooteka ("He Puts away the Drum"). Sam became a favorite of Oolooteka, known to the whites as Old Jolly. Sam became known as "The Raven" to the Indians, a name thought to have been given to him by Oolooteka. Being aware of his own family history, it is more likely he took the name from the ravens in his family coat-of arms. Oolooteka was a popular Cherokee chief, but some of his success has been attributed to his brother-in-law, John Rogers, who was part Scot. This Scottish link could have been responsible for the special bond between Houston and his Cherokee brethren. Sam Houston started his military career on March 24th, 1813, when, at the age of 20, he took a silver dollar from a drumhead and enlisted in the Regular Army, until March 1st, 1818, when he resigned. By 1821, he had begun his political career in Lebanon, Tennessee starting off as a young lawyer and eventually serving as District Attorney, Adjutant General and State Congressman. In 1827, he was elected Governor. In 1829, he resigned as Governor and in 1832 he went to Texas to report on Indian affairs for Andrew Jackson. In 1833, he signed the Texas Declaration of Independence and was elected Commander-in-Chief of the armies.

Houston led the Battle of San Jacinto April 21, 1836, where the Mexicans suffered 630 killed, 208 wounded and 730 captured, including General Santa Anna. He proudly led his band of 900 men into battle to the tune of "Will You Come to the Bower" played by one drummer and one fifer. His army overran the Mexican army of 1400 in only eighteen minutes. The Texan losses were minimal with only two killed and some minor injuries including Houston, who was shot in the ankle. This defeat led to the elimination of Mexican control under Santa Anna and the establishment of Texas as an independent territory.

After recovering from his wounds received at the battle of San Jacinto, Houston was elected President of the new Republic of Texas and was re-elected to a second term as President in 1840. After serving two terms as President, he served Texas as a senator for almost 14 years and favored annexation to the United States. He was re-elected as Governor in 1859 and opposed the secession of Texas. He was eventually deposed at the secession convention and refused the aid of union forces to keep his position. He retired to Houston, and in 1845 moved 14 miles east of Huntsville, to a plantation he called "Raven Hill". In 1848, he moved his family to Huntsville, where he lived until his death.

General Sam Houston died in 1863 at the age of 70.

David Crockett

> *Loved to have his ears tickled by tales of his descent*
> - Sir Walter Scott, *Ivanhoe*

David "Davy" Crockett was born August 17, 1786, in what is now Tennessee. His own ancestors are unclear of the family's lineage; however, in *Three Roads to the Alamo*, William Davis writes that Crockett's ancestors were surely Scottish, most likely part of the Scotch-Irish migration to America. In his autobiography,

Davy Crockett writes that his father was either born in Ireland, or was born during the passage from Ireland to America. David Crockett's father, John, fought during the American Revolution at King's Mountain against the British, who were under the command of Major Patrick Ferguson, born in Aberdeen, Scotland, who developed a breech loading rifle.

By the time Crockett arrived in Texas in 1835, he was already an American icon, thanks in part to books and almanacs put out by the Whig party. During his political career, members of the Whig party capitalized upon his folksy humor and backwoods ways in a series of publications. These did much to promote his image, however they did not help him while serving in Congress. Crockett had a poor record in Congress, his political career was going nowhere, he butted heads with Polk, and argued with his own party members. No bills he introduced were ever passed, most of which had to do with land acquisitions.

Reasons for Crockett to be in Texas

After his congressional defeat in 1835, losing to Adam Huntsman, a peg-legged lawyer supported by Crockett's one time mentor turned nemesis, Andrew Jackson, Crockett made a toast to some friends saying, "Since you have chosen to elect a man with a timber toe to succeed me, you may all go to hell and I will go to Texas."

Crockett made his way to Texas seeking land to provide a source of affluence for his family, and hoping to rejuvenate his political career, as seen in his last letter to his family dated January 9, 1836:

> "…I have taken the oath of government and have enrolled my name as a volunteer and will set out for the Rio Grand in a few days with the volunteers from the United States. But all volunteers is entitled to vote for a member of the convention or to be voted for, and I have but little doubt of being elected a member to form a constitution for this province. I am rejoiced at my fate. I have rather be in my present situation than to be

elected to a seat in Congress for life. I am in hopes of making a fortune yet for myself and family, bad as my prospect has been."

The reasons as to why Crockett was at the Alamo during Santa Anna's siege are uncertain. At that time in Texas, the territory was split into two political factions, those supporting a conservative Whig philosophy (favoring a republic) and those supporting the administration of Andrew Jackson. Crockett chose to join Col. William B. Travis rather than support Houston, a Jackson sympathizer.

Crockett's Coonskin Cap

Some questions arise as to whether Crockett really wore a coonskin cap. Susanna Dickinson, Alamo survivor and wife of one of the defenders, made reference to his "peculiar cap" beside his body when she was brought out of the church to the courtyard. His daughter recalls him leaving Tennessee in 1835 on his way to Texas with his rifle and wearing his coonskin cap. James D. Davis years later recalls Crockett leaving Memphis stating that Crockett "wore that same veritable coon-skin cap and hunting shirt, bearing upon his shoulder his ever faithful rifle."

Crockett's Fiddle Playing

The instruments we associate with Scotland in the time period of 1600-1800 are the bagpipes, the fiddle and the harp. Both the bagpipes and the fiddle represented Scotland at the Alamo. Fidil, fythil and the fedyl are among the early spellings of the fiddle, and along with a similar instrument called a rebec or rybid it was an instrument played with a bow. With the arrival of other stringed instruments from France and other European countries called viols, said to have been invented in the 1500s, Scottish musicians and instrument makers were quick to see the potential of these instruments for their national music. Basically this is where the names fiddle and violin come from. They are now the same instrument but are referred to as one or the other according to the type of music played: folk (traditional) or fine (classical).

Many references occur concerning the devil and fiddle playing in the Southern states and it's said Auld Nick himself was a fiddler. The devil is referred to as Auld Nick in Scotland. This goes back to Scotland, when, for religious reasons, music and dance were banned by the church, especially music on the fiddle. Once again we experience the old superstitions and religious beliefs from Scotland indoctrinated into the lives of the early American settlers. Many fiddle tunes and songs have been written for, to and about the devil in Scotland, Ireland and the States.

Both Susanna Dickinson and Madame Candelaria, who claimed to have been inside the Alamo, nursing Jim Bowie, recall Crockett playing the fiddle. However, on the subject of David Crockett as a fiddle player I have to throw another spanner in the works, so to speak. I don't believe he played fiddle. This subject was brought to my attention by a prominent Alamo historian and published author, Dr. Bruce Winders. It seems the first mention of Crockett ever having played the fiddle was from Susanna Dickinson in her interviews after the Alamo's fall. It is never mentioned anywhere before, not even by Crockett himself in the only authentic autobiography written by him, that being *A Narrative of the Life of David Crockett of Tennessee written by himself.* All others, including *An Account of Colonel Crockett's Exploits and Adventures in Texas* and *An Account of Colonel Crockett's Tour to the North and Down East* have proven to be hoaxes written by others after his death. Even these publications make no mention of his playing the fiddle. Why would Crockett himself not have mentioned it, or for that matter, anyone who ever knew him before? Thomas Jefferson was a fiddler and ample mention of his fiddle playing is written down. Why not Crockett's?

For a man who was so much in the public eye and who enjoyed good times you would think it would have been a notable and noticeable action. Travis did not mention it, although he did draw attention to Crockett's influence and his positive attitude in keeping the men's spirits high. Travis wrote a fair amount of information in his letters pertaining to the situation, but nary a word about Crockett's fiddle. It's true he never wrote about any music being played, but maybe it was just because it was such a common occurrence with the men, and even the Mexicans had a fair amount of music going on. I think though, if Crockett had played fiddle, Travis would have noticed.

I can only draw one conclusion. Susanna Dickinson mistook Micajah Autry for Crockett. Autry has been described as a sensitive man, an amateur poet, writer, artist and musician. Autry rode in with Crockett from Nacogdoches as did MacGregor the piper. MacGregor and Autry most probably knew each other beforehand, and possibly played music together. Susanna described Crockett as being 5ft 10ins tall or taller. Most other sources have Crockett being around 5ft 8ins. Autry was 5ft 10ins. Autry was also a designated sharpshooter, another reason he could have been mistaken for Crockett. Perhaps they looked alike, in spite of the height difference. Their ages were close, Autry being 42 and Crockett 49.

I'm aware that there is a fiddle in the Witte Museum in San Antonio and that there is a claim that it could be Crockett's fiddle. Let's look at that story and consider other possibilities. In 1933, a violin builder by the name of T.S. Quinn tried to sell a fiddle to the Mayor of San Antonio, Judge C.K. Quin. T.S. Quinn eventually gave the fiddle to the mayor. Quinn claims he bought the instrument from a Frank Hollis. Frank's father, Tom Hollis, allegedly received it from David Crockett's son in Franklin County, Tennessee in 1859. Inside the fiddle is written "This fiddle is my property, Davy Crockett, Franklin County, Tenn. Feb 14, 1819". It was not in David Crockett's own hand-writing and he always referred to himself as David, not Davy. Both Quinn and Hollis gave affidavits attesting to the truthfulness of their statements, but no such affidavit was given by Crockett's son. Even if it was David's fiddle, something he owned, once again, why no mention of him ever having played it? Crockett was hardly a Texian at the time of his death, and it was not initially his intent to become involved with the revolution, but his death at the Alamo seemed tailor-made for such an American icon. Anything belonging to Crockett would be of immediate value as souvenirs. For example, 20 horses were sold back east, each sale claiming to be the very horse that David Crockett rode into Texas on. There are many references to David's fiddle playing, but only after Susanna's mention of it years later. Even Madame Candelaria's statements are after the fact, and

Susanna claims that Madame Candelaria was not even in the Alamo. To sum it up, I don't think Crockett ever played the fiddle, but the playing could be attributed to Micajah Autry. His repertoire was most likely made up of the Scottish tunes brought over to the American South during the Scotch-Irish migration.

Crockett's Death

The facts surrounding Crockett's death are also uncertain. Susanna Dickinson said that Crockett died on the outside, one of the earliest to fall. Travis' slave and the only male Texan to survive the battle, reported seeing Crockett lying dead with slain Mexicans around him and stated that only one man, named Warner, surrendered to the Mexicans. Another report by one of Santa Anna's men, Lt. Jose Enrique de la Peña, in his diary published in 1975, stated that Crockett and five or six others were captured by the Mexican troops and taken to the Alamo courtyard, even though Santa Anna had issued orders to take no prisoners. The angry general ordered them executed immediately. They were bayoneted and shot, but their reputations remained intact. De la Peña described in his diary that "these unfortunates died without complaining and without humiliating themselves before their torturers." Still another story says that Crockett did not surrender but was caught trying to escape. In the last minutes of the battle a handful of defenders were driven back into the main mission building. They took refuge in one of the rooms of the long barracks and tried to hide under a stack of buffalo robes. These men were caught and brought into the forecourt. One of the Mexican generals pleaded for their cause but Santa Anna, who ordered his soldiers to carry out his original orders to spare no one, dismissed his efforts.

Whatever the manner of his actions and death, David "Davy" Crockett cemented his place in American history by fighting for freedom at the Alamo. His memorial marker reads: "Davy Crockett, Pioneer, Patriot, Soldier, Trapper, Explorer, State Legislator, Congressman, Martyred at The Alamo. 1786-1836."

At the time of his death on March 6, 1836 David Crockett was 49 years old.

More on Micajah Autry (pronounced Mi-kay'-cha)

Born in Sampson County, North Carolina in 1794, Micajah was known to be an excellent marksmen. During the siege he was chosen by his company to eliminate Santa Anna, who often strolled across the grounds just beyond the Alamo walls. He missed his mark and Santa Anna never gave him the opportunity again although it was said that other Mexican soldiers fell victim to his marksmanship. In a later report, a Mexican soldier recalled this sharpshooter's name as Kockie, thus sprouting the believe that it was probably Crockett, but the pronunciation of Autry by a Mexican could very well sound like Kockie. In Autry's birthplace of Sampson County, settlers first started arriving around 1740. It was densely wooded and had a large deer population for hunting, where a man could develop his skills with a rifle. In Sampson County there is a town called Ivanhoe (named after one of Scott's novels), close by Autry's birthplace. The first pastor at the Black River Presbyterian Church, in Ivanhoe, was from Scotland. Services were given in Gaelic for many years indicating a large Highland population. The area also contained many Scotch-Irish. Autry would have been brought up listening to Scottish music and surrounded by folks steeped in Scottish tradition and speaking with Scottish accents.

John Hubbard Forsyth

It is worth a few words here to mention John Hubbard Forsyth who may have been third in command after Bowie and Travis and who would have had the last command in the final stages of the battle when Travis went down early. Forsyth was the commanding officer of cavalry company KIB and traveled with his men, accompanying Travis to the Alamo. Forsyth had come to Texas from Kentucky in 1835, having left his father's farm in Avon, New York in 1828. Forsyth's ancestry can be traced as far back as 1640, to his great-great-great-great-grandfather Gilbert Forsyth, who was born in Ballindollach, Scotland and emigrated to the Colonies and died in Hartford, Connecticut.

Son: James Forsyth Sr., born.1670 Hartford, CT; died ? Groton, CT.
Son: James Forsyth Jr., born June 12th 1711 Groton/New London, CT; died 1760 Chesterfield, CT.
Son: Jonathan Forsyth, born 1740, Hadden Neck, CT; died 1788 Geneva, NY.
Son: Alexander Forsyth, born Sept 9th, 1772 in Wyoming, PA or CT; died May 25th 1846, Rochester, New York.
Son: John Hubbard Forsyth, born Aug 10th 1797 in Avon, Livingston Co., New York; died March 6th, 1836, at The Alamo.

Jonathon Forsyth was killed by Indians in 1788. His daughter reported in a statement made on February 20th, 1854: "My father moved to Geneva, in three or four years and he died there in 1788..... My father went first to Wilkes Barre to mill and when father came back (to Wyoming, PA), the Shawnee attacked him, burnt his hay stack. He fled to his canoe and sunk himself into the water from time to time as they fired nine rounds at him. Next day he could not swim". This information was passed on to me by my friend Linda Adair who herself is part of the Forsyth family tree. Her contact, clan Forsyth genealogist Edward Forsyth, has quite a record of the large family of Forsyths. One of the Forsyth family members named his estate in Dundas, Ontario, after the ancestral home in Ballindollach, Scotland, which helped them trace their roots.

James Bowie

> "Raise me from my bed," said the invalid; "throw my plaid around me, and bring me my claymore, dirk and pistols; it shall never be said that a foeman saw Rob Roy MacGregor defenseless and unarmed."
> - Sir Walter Scott, *Rob Roy*

James Bowie was born in the spring of 1796 in a part of Kentucky that is now Tennessee. The Bowie clan is from Sterlingshire on the edge of the Scottish Highlands. The name is derived from the Gaelic Buidhe. The

Bowies originated in the Inner Hebrides and later moved inland through Argyle to Inverness.

Jim Bowie's name perpetuated the Bowie tradition of honoring King James VI of Scotland. Since the mid-1580s James VI had provided a house in Cowper to "Jerome Bowie, Master of the King's Wines". The Bowies were also guards of the royal household in the 15th century. Bowie's grandfather, also James, came to Maryland in 1742 and fought in the Revolutionary War.

There is some speculation that the Bowies were also relatives of the famous Rob Roy MacGregor. If this holds any truth there would have been two of clan Gregor who died at the Alamo. The MacGregors were an outlawed clan, first proscribed in 1604 by James VI and almost continually until 1775. Rob Roy and his MacGregors were known to steal cattle and sell them back to their original owners, or to offer protection against cattle stealing.

Before the revolution in Texas, Bowie led an adventurous life. He searched for gold and silver in Texas and befriended Indians along the way. He became fairly rich at an early age while in business with two of his brothers, Rezin and John. They had dealings in sugar milling, land speculation and slave trading. The land speculation involved large tracts in Arkansas, to which they did not possess title. The slave trading was a money-laundering scheme for the pirate Jean LaFitte. LaFitte would smuggle slaves into the country through the Bowie brothers who would then inform on themselves and collect half of what the "contraband property" would bring at auction as a reward. The buyers at the auction were usually themselves and they would then resell the victims for a profit. A comparison could be made between Rob Roy and his alleged descendant.

The famous Bowie knife, that James Bowie is so closely identified with, was actually designed by his brother Rezin from a file he gave to a blacksmith. However, James made it famous when he used it to disembowel a man during a duel that turned into a brawl. This knife that Bowie adopted could be, in spirit, if not design, descended from the fierce Scottish dirks.

Reasons for Bowie to be in Texas

James Bowie went to Texas with his brothers, arriving in San Antonio in 1828, in search of a fortune. Most of the time he was in financial troubles, as his land schemes had been thwarted by the authorities. When Texas started to open up outside the authority of the U.S., he saw an opportunity to start over, and expected to amass a fortune in his Texas ventures.

Bowie married Ursula Veramendi, who was the daughter of the man who was governor of the province of Texas and vice-governor of the Mexican state of Coahuila y Texas. Sources disagree about how many children they had, ranging from zero to two; however, when he was away on a business trip, cholera hit the family, killing all. When he returned to San Antonio and found his family gone he began to drink heavily.

When war broke out, Texas refused to give him a commission, however, Sam Houston found him useful and treated him as a colonel based on his ranger service for Veramendi against the Comanches. He proved a successful and popular leader in several skirmishes before the Alamo. One of his men, Noah Smithwick, recalled years later that he "never needlessly spent a bullet or imperiled a life. His voice is still ringing in my old deaf ears as he repeatedly admonished us. 'Keep under cover boys and reserve your fire; we haven't a man to spare.'"

Bowie arrived at the Alamo on January 19, 1836 with a detachment of thirty men. Shortly after arriving, Col. James C. Neill, commander, left the Alamo for family business, leaving Travis in charge. The volunteers preferred to follow Bowie and demanded an election. On February 13th, Travis and Bowie came to a compromise leaving the command of the

Texas regulars and cavalry to Travis, and the command of the volunteers to Bowie, both men sharing joint authority and correspondence duties. On February 24th, Bowie collapsed, suffering from what is thought to be pneumonia or advanced tuberculosis. He was confined to his cot and urged his men to follow Travis. When the attack occurred on the Alamo, Bowie was on his cot in a room on the south side of the mission. He was found dead with several bullet wounds to the head. A friend of his, Caiaphas K. Ham, described him as: "...a clever, polite gentleman...attentive to the ladies on all occasions ... a true, constant, and generous friend ...a foe no one dared to undervalue and many feared."

At the time of his death on March 6, 1836 Bowie was 39 years old.

William Barrett Travis

> *Our numbers are few but activity and courage may supply that defect.*
> - Sir Walter Scott, *Ivanhoe*

William Barrett Travis, born August 1809 in South Carolina, was a descendant of Travers of Tulketh Castle, near Preston, England. His father, Berwick Travers, unlike Bowie's and Crockett's fathers, seemed to have missed the American Revolution. Travis became an attorney, married, had a son, published a newspaper and joined the militia, all in his early 20s. Travis left his son and pregnant wife and went to Texas in 1831. There is reason to believe that Travis' wife had a lover, for he never really acknowledged his daughter as he did his son. Once in Texas, he set up a law practice and joined the Texas forces. Shortly before the Texas Revolution began, his wife showed up with the two children to ask for a divorce.

Travis, a lawyer and avid reader, had among his favorite books Sir Walter Scott's *Ivanhoe*, *Waverley* and *The Black Dwarf*, and Jane Porter's *The*

Scottish Chiefs, a novel about William Wallace. He also read Lord Byron, an English author who spent eight years of his early life in Scotland.

To many, it seemed that Travis emulated the heroes in these novels. An example can be found in Sir Walter Scott's novel *Waverley* when the main character, a young colonel, Edward Waverley from England, gets caught up in the Jacobite cause of 1745-46, when Prince Charles Edward Stewart tried to regain the Scottish crown for his father. It became a lost cause ending in the Battle of Culloden in 1746. By coincidence or not, Travis' son was called Charles Edward, possibly after both characters in the novel.

Reasons for Travis to be in Texas

Of the three most famous names, Travis was more involved in Texas politics than Crockett or Bowie. He was running from debt and took advantage of the agreement with Mexico in 1824 for a new start and to receive a tract of land. By this time, Steve Austin was having a hard time keeping the 1824 agreement in place. Eventually he gave up and sided with the others who saw Texas becoming a republic. Travis must have influenced Austin in this decision, as the Mexicans knew Travis as a troublemaker. Some saw him as a leader, and towards that end he envisioned himself victorious over the Mexicans.

On orders from Provisional Governor Henry Smith in January 1836, Travis went to the Alamo with approximately 30 men. As mentioned before, Bowie and Travis agreed upon a compromise of duties. It was a strained truce, one that favored Bowie, but Travis eventually gained full command when Bowie became ill. Travis is usually unfairly portrayed as a pompous officer, one whom the volunteers refused to follow. However, Travis was outgoing and well-liked by his peers. Bowie's election had more to do with the fact that the volunteers preferred to take orders from one of their own rather than a regular officer of the Texas Army. There is no doubt that Travis was in charge and he was confident that fame and glory would be theirs. He saw the situation as win-win; either they would have victory and glory, or death and glory. Crockett is usually credited with keeping up the men's spirits with his stories and behavior but it was

Travis who inspired confidence and hope. Travis tried in vain to gain public support and enlist more volunteers for their cause. It has been estimated the Mexican force numbered between 2,400 and 5,000 to Travis' 189 men. He and his greatly outnumbered force held off the Mexican army as long as possible, vowing to defend the Alamo until death - which they did. It is estimated the Mexicans lost approximately 1600 in the battle. The only survivors on the Texian side were 16 women and children who had gone to the Alamo for refuge.

At the time of his death on March 6, 1836 William B. Travis was 26 years old.

Line in the Sand

A famous story from inside the Alamo is that of the "line in the sand". It is reported that Travis, recognizing how grave the situation was, on the 3rd of March drew a line in the sand with his sword and asked that every defender willing to fight to the death cross over. All but one crossed vowing to fight to the end, and even the ailing Bowie instructed his men to carry his cot across the line. 26-year-old Tapley Holland was reportedly the first to cross. Louis "Moses" Rose apparently did not.

The story was told to a couple called the Zubers many years later after Moses Rose escaped and turned up at their home in Gonzales, where Rose told the story. The Zubers, in turn, passed it on to their son, who embellished it beyond credibility. He later admitted to embellishing the story but still claimed that most of it was true. Many historians have debated whether this event occurred on the first or last day of the siege or if it even happened at all. The "line in the sand" story was later brought to the attention of Susannah Dickinson who was at the Alamo during the attack. She remembered something of this sort happening, but was unclear of the details. Enrique Esparza, who was also present inside the Alamo, and whose father died in the fight, also recalls the incident. In an interview dated May 12th, & 19th, 1907 he states "Rose went out after Travis drew the line with his sword. He was the only man who did not cross the line. Up to then he had fought as brave as any man there. He stood by the cannon. Rose went out during the night. They opened a window for him and let him go. The others who left before went out of the doors and in the daytime." Esparza was referring to a three-day armistice Santa Anna had granted during the siege.

Andrea Castanon Villanueva, more commonly known as Madame Candelaria, in an interview dated February 19th, 1899 states "One evening Colonel Travis made a fine speech to his soldiers." Madame Candelaria does not pretend to remember what he said, but she does remember he drew a line on the floor with the point of his sword and asked all those who were willing to die for Texas to come over to his side. They all quickly stepped across the line but two men. One of these sprang over the wall and disappeared. The other was Bowie who, as stated before, was carried across. Susanna Dickinson says that Madame Candelaria was not in the Alamo and Esparza says "I do not remember seeing Madame Candelaria there. She may have been among the women and I may not have noticed her particularly. She claimed to have been there and I will not dispute her word. I did not notice the women as closely as I did the men." The Texas legislature did appoint a committee to investigate her claims and concluded that after examining witnesses and going over the records in the old mission, she was indeed in the Alamo and looked after Bowie. Many, however, still do not believe that Madame Candelaria was at the Alamo.

Did Travis draw a line in the sand? The debate goes on. Alan C. Huffines, in his book, *Blood of Noble Men*, writes "Historians generally do not want to believe that something this melodramatic happened." There was no one more melodramatic involved in the whole scenario than Travis. Consider the letters he wrote:

> People of Texas and all Americans in the World —
>
> Fellow citizens & compatriots —
>
> I am besieged, by a thousand or more of the Mexicans under Anna- I have sustained a continual Bombardment & cannonade

for 24hours & have not lost a man — The enemy has demanded a surrender at discretion, otherwise, the garrison are to be put to the sword, if the fort is taken - I have answered the demand with a cannon shot, & our flag still waves proudly from the walls - I shall never surrender or retreat. Then, I call on you in the name of Liberty, of patriotism & every thing dear to the American character, to come to our aid, with all dispatch - The enemy is receiving reinforcements daily & will no doubt increase to three or four thousand in four or five days. If this call is neglected, I am determined to sustain myself as long as possible & die a soldier who never forgets what is due to his own honor & that of his country -

    VICTORY OR DEATH
    - William Barret Travis, Lt. Col. Comdt.

and to David Ayres, who was caring for Travis' son:

"Take care of my little boy. If the country may be saved I may make for him a splendid fortune; but if the country be lost and I should perish, he will have nothing but the proud recollection that he is the son of a man who died for his country."

Also consider the events of May 1832. One of Santa Anna's commanders in Anahuac, Texas, Col. Bradburn, had Travis and Patrick C. Jack arrested for being troublemakers. They were confined in brick kilns, which had been transformed into prisons. On June 10th, a rescue attempt was made after negotiations to free them had broken down. Bradburn gave orders that the prisoners were to be bound and shot at the first sign of an attack. The prisoners were tied down to the ground and the Mexican soldiers stood over them with muskets poised. Travis, aware of what was going on, and sensing that Austin and some of his men might be within hearing distance, shouted to them to forget about him and "blaze away upon the fort." The Texians outside the kiln found his words moving, and were impressed that Travis never shrunk but called on his friends to witness that he would die like a man. Col Bradburn, perhaps to avoid any actual skirmish, then released Travis and Jack.

In another event, on September 12th, 1835, Austin was elected chairman of a meeting that suggested that a consultation of all Texas was imperative, reaffirming loyalty to the 1824 constitution. Each jurisdiction was to send 5 delegates. On October 15th, the convention was called for in San Felipe. On October 3rd, Mexican troops appeared outside Gonzales where about 150 Texian volunteers were on hand to confront them. Travis, with his friend Henry Smith and other members of the elected delegates, in the company of an army of about 300, were on their way to Bexar. Because of this, not enough delegates appeared for Austin's convention and it was postponed until November 1st. While waiting for Bowie and Fannin, Travis and the other delegates took a vote to determine a course of action. Travis wanted to remain with the army, while most of the others felt they should continue on to take their seats at the convention. Austin paraded the command in order to hear views on the issue. Volunteers voted that the delegates should go to San Felipe, while Travis declined.

In searching for other facts as to whether or not the line in the sand actually happened, we could look at another similar incident, which occurred before the Travis line. A precedent had already been set in late 1835 when General Cos of the Mexican Army was in San Antonio with 1400 troops. The Texans approached San Antonio on October 27th, and settled in for a siege. When the conditions in the Texan camp began to disintegrate, their resolve began to crumble under the waiting, and the chill of the early December weather. In a council of war, the field officers voted to withdraw the volunteers. Ben Milam was one volunteer in the Texan camp who disagreed with the plan, knowing that the Mexican moral was also cracking. Milam was a Welshman from Kentucky who had been involved in Texas affairs even before Austin. The idea of walking away from the enemy was particularly upsetting. He expressed his views by drawing a line in the dust with his rifle and shouting, "Who will go with old Ben Milam into San Antonio? Who will follow old Ben Milam?" On the morning of December 5, 1835, some 300 Texans drove into San Antonio with Milam in command. This story was surely repeated time and again around San Antonio and the Alamo, and it must have been on Travis' mind when he presented his challenge to his men.

It is generally accepted by most historians that when Travis realized that no help was coming, he called the men together and offered them three choices: surrender, escape or fight to the death. Did he draw a line in the sand at this point? It is still a subject for debate, but does seem credible. There are several points that seem too true to be made up:
1. The report of a similar incident when Milam drew a line in the sand with his rifle;
2. Travis reportedly drew the line with his sword. This seems plausible since Travis was one of the few at the Alamo with a sword, others carried rifles, knives and an occasional tomahawk;
3. The detail of carrying Bowie's cot over the line also seems consistent As a co-leader of the men he would have wanted to support the majority vote and as a Texas landowner he would have wanted to defend his land to the death rather than see it go under the rule of the despised dictator Santa Anna. Even though Bowie was physically unable to fight, the act of carrying his cot over the line gave the men a huge morale boost.
4. To recall and actually name Tapley Holland as the first to cross also seems like a detail too unlikely just to make up for credibility's sake.

Earlier during the siege Travis had already stated his position, to fight to the death. It seems reasonable that he would offer this to his men in such a dramatic way as drawing a line in the sand.

> *"What remains," asks Rebecca "when death has broken the strong man's spear and overtaken the speed of his warhorse."*
> *"What remains?" cried Ivanhoe. "Glory, maiden, glory which gilds our sepulchre and embalms our name.*
>   - Sir Walter Scott, *Ivanhoe*

Moses Rose

Early historians raised some doubt as to whether there was a man called "Rose" at the Alamo, because there was also a "Ross" present. It was thought that they may have been the same person, with a misspelling in early records. Since then, the fact has been established that Moses Rose was at the Alamo, and was a separate identity from Ross, and that he did escape and made his way to Nacogdoches has also been established. He himself gave an account of the "line drawn in the sand." Although questioned many years later he seemed to be less certain of what happened. This seems reasonable, that during the passage of time some of what happened may be less easily remembered.

Louis (Moses) Rose was born on May 11, 1785, in Laferée, Ardennes, France. He was a soldier of fortune who fought with Napoleon, and in the French Legion of Honor. He served in Naples, Portugal, Spain and Russia. He eventually settled in Nacogdoches, Texas, about 1827. He worked as a log cutter and hauler and also served as a messenger between Nacogdoches and Natchitoches, Louisiana. He took part in the battle of Nacogdoches in 1832 and the siege of Bexar in 1835. Rose had arrived at the Alamo in the Autumn of 1835 with friend, Jim Bowie. At that time he was 51 years old, and this earned him the nickname, Moses.

It is said that when asked, "Moses, why didn't you stay there in the Alamo with the others?" he invariably replied, "By God, I wasn't ready to die."

In 1842 he moved to Logansport, Louisiana, where he lived until his death. At the time of his death in 1851, Moses Rose was 66 years old.

John MacGregor

> *All is possible for those who dare to die.*
> - Sir Walter Scott, *Ivanhoe*

John MacGregor, born in Scotland in 1808, will be remembered forever as the piper of the Alamo. According to Susanna Dickinson, MacGregor played the pipes and staged musical duets with a fiddler whom she identified as Davy Crockett, at times trying to out-do each other in noise rather than in musical ability. Although nothing is known of John MacGregor's birthplace in Scotland, he had a Highland name, and the pipes certainly are a Highland instrument. It was not uncommon for folks to bring their musical instruments with them, and many tales are told of the pipers playing laments as the ships left for their journeys across the ocean. There is some indication that he may have hailed from near Perth. He was difficult to understand when he spoke, either from having a thick brogue, or perhaps he spoke Gaelic. He may also have been a victim of the Highland Clearances, when so many Highlanders were forced to leave their homes and emigrate to North America. It is known that he took part in the siege and battle at Bexar and received a donation certificate for 640 acres for his participation. He was 2nd Sergeant in Captain Carey's Artillery Company. He may have remained in Bexar or returned for a short time to his residence in Nacogdoches to eventually accompany Crockett, and his Tennessee Volunteers, back to the Alamo. The whereabouts of MacGregor's bagpipes have never been determined.

At the time of his death on March 6, 1836 John MacGregor was 28 years old.

Other Scots at the Alamo

The knights are dust and their good swords are rust, their souls are with the saints, we trust.
    - Sir Walter Scott, *Ivanhoe*

Three of the other Alamo defenders: Richard W. Ballentine, Isaac Robinson, David L. Wilson were also from Scotland.

Richard W. Ballentine was born in Scotland in 1814. His residence was Alabama but he sailed for Texas arriving in December 1835. He and the other passengers signed a statement declaring, "we have left every endearment at our respective places of abode in the United States of America, to maintain and defend our brethren, at the peril of our lives, liberties and fortunes." His rank was that of a private (rifleman).

At the time of his death on March 6, 1836 Richard W. Ballentine was 22 years old.

Isaac Robinson was born in Scotland in 1808 and came to Texas from Louisiana. He took part in the siege of Bexar and later served in the Alamo garrison as a fourth sergeant in Capt. William R. Carey's artillery company.

At the time of his death on March 6, 1836 Isaac Robinson was 28 years old.

David L. Wilson, son of James and Susanna (Wesley) Wilson, was born in Scotland in 1807. In Texas he lived in Nacogdoches with his wife, Ophelia. Wilson was probably one of the volunteers who accompanied Capt. Philip Dimmitt to Bexar and the Alamo in the early months of 1836. He remained at the Alamo after Dimmitt left on the first day of the siege.

At the time of his death on March 6, 1836 David L. Wilson was 29 years old.

General Antonio López de Santa Anna

Who was Gen. Santa Anna? If there is a villain in this scenario, it is certainly Santa Anna. He was a very controversial figure during his time and remains so today. He was a self-styled dictator and thought of himself as the "Napoleon of the West." He was born February 21st, 1794 to middle class Spanish parents in Vera Cruz. At 16, he became a cadet in an infantry unit, policing Indian tribes and in 1829, he became known as the "hero of Tampico" when he helped to defeat an invading Spanish army. He became president of Mexico for the first time in 1833. His centralist policies were unpopular and led to rebellions in several regions. He led his army against the rebellion in the Texas territory in 1836, when he defeated the men at the Alamo. He later lost Texas after his defeat at San Jacinto. After the battle, Santa Anna was captured and brought before Gen. Sam Houston. It is said he gave the secret Master Mason distress signal and Houston, a fellow Mason, honored it, letting Santa Anna live.

Santa Anna returned to Mexico and helped defend his country against the French in 1838, where he lost a leg in combat. In 1839, he became acting president and dictator from 1841 to 1845. He was overthrown for his excesses and was exiled to Cuba. He returned to Mexico during the Mexican-American War to take command of the Mexican forces, but was defeated by Zachary Taylor at the Battle of Buena Vista, and by Winfield Scott at the Battle of Cerro Gordo. After the fall of Mexico City, he returned to exile but was called back by conservatives to head the government from 1853 to 1855. He was again overthrown for selling the Mesilla Valley to the United States as the Gadsden Purchase. He was allowed to return to Mexico City in 1874 where he lived out the rest of his life.

He died in obscurity June 20, 1876 at the age of 82.

Captain Ewen Cameron

Ewen Cameron was born in Scotland about 1811. He was named for the Scottish hero Sir Ewen Cameron of Lochiel, Laird of Clan Cameron, who was a staunch supporter of King Charles II. Cameron traveled to Texas during the Texas Revolution and served two terms in the Texas army. On October 20th, 1836, he reenlisted as a private in Capt. Clark L. Owen's Company A of Joseph H. D. Rogers' First Regiment, Permanent Volunteers. He served until the company was mustered out on December 31st, 1836. For his service, he received bounty warrants for a total of 1,920 acres, which his heirs later claimed in San Patricio County. In the period that followed the revolution, he won renown as a leader of the "cowboys", prominent in frontier defense in South Texas. The Telegraph and Texas Register hailed him on September 14, 1842, as "a bold and chivalrous leader" who promised to become "the Bruce of the West."

On July 7, 1842, Cameron took part in the battle of Lipantitlán against Gen. Antonio Canales. Samuel H. Walker attributed much of the credit for the successful defense of the position to Cameron. At the battle of Mier, "The fearless Cameron, whose company garrisoned the back yard of one of the houses, being charged by an imposing force of the enemy, after emptying his rifles into their lines, beat off the foe until he could reload, with the loose stones in the court." At Pass Suarte, after Fisher and the staff officers had been separated from the command, the Mier prisoners unanimously chose Cameron as their commander. On Saturday, February 19, Cameron and about sixty men were recaptured by Mexicans and subjected with other groups to the Black Bean Episode. Cameron drew a white bean in the lottery meaning his life was spared, but was later shot by a firing squad for a subsequent attempt at escape. It is said he refused a blindfold, saying "For the liberty of Texas, Ewen Cameron can look death in the face!"

Influence of Sir Walter Scott, Robert Burns and Lord Byron

Sir Walter Scott (1771-1832) Novelist, Poet and Songwriter. Born in Edinburgh, Scotland.
Robert Burns (1759- 1796) Poet and Songwriter. Born in Ayrshire, Scotland.
George Gordon Byron (1788-1824) Poet. Born in England.

All three figured prominently in the readings of both William Travis and Sam Houston and probably in the readings of most Americans at that time, especially the families of Austin's original settlers, for they were handpicked by Austin for certain qualities which included literacy. Over ninety percent were said to be literate and well educated folks, as well as being hard working and willing.

Sir Walter Scott is said to have put chivalry and romance into the Southern states through his Waverley novels, a series of novels so named from the first of them published in 1807. They were very popular throughout the States but especially in the South where they would be read by folks who could understand and recognize their heritage. He was Travis' favorite author and Travis was known to have borrowed three of Scott's novels one winter. Among Scott's works known to have been read by Travis were *Ivanhoe*, *The Black Dwarf* and *Waverley*. The most intriguing of these would seem to be *Waverley*. It is the story of a young English officer who joins the Highland Jacobite army of Bonnie Prince Charlie to fight the Government forces of King George II made up of Scottish and English troops. In essence, two different cultures facing off. Following are some excerpts from *Waverley*, from a battle scene as the Jacobite and Government armies face off. Note the similarities between this battle scene and that of the Alamo. Remember too that Travis of English ancestry finds himself fighting with folks of mostly Scottish ancestry.

"Here, then, was a military spectacle of no ordinary interest or usual oral occurrence. The two armies, so different in aspect and discipline, yet each admirably trained in its own peculiar mode of war, upon whose conflict the temporary fate at least of Scotland appeared to depend, now faced each other like two gladiators in the arena, each meditating upon the mode of attacking the enemy. The leading officers and the general's staff of each Army could be distinguished in front of their lines, busied with spy-glasses to watch each other's motions, and occupied in despatching the orders and receiving the intelligence conveyed by the aides-de-camp and orderly men, who gave life to the scene by galloping along in different directions, as if the fate of the day depended upon the speed of their horses. The space between the armies was at times occupied by the partial and irregular contest of individual sharpshooters, and a hat or bonnet was occasionally seen to fall, as the wounded man was borne off by his comrades. These, however, were but trifling scrimmages, for it suited the views of neither party to advance in that direction."

"Almost at the same instant the van of the English appeared issuing from among the trees and inclosures of Seaton, with the purpose of occupying the level plain between the high ground and the sea; the space which divided the armies being only about half a mile in breadth, Waverley could plainly see the squadrons all of the dragoons issue, one after another, from the defiles, with their viddettes in front, and form upon the plain, with their front opposed to that all the Prince's army. They were followed by a train of field-pieces, which, when they reached the flank of the dragoons, were also brought into line and pointed against the heights. The march was continued by three or four regiments of infantry marching in open column, their fixed bayonets showing like successive hedges of steel, and their arms glancing like lightning, as, at the signal given, they also at once wheeled up, and were placed in direct opposition to the Highlanders. A second train of artillery, with another regiment of horse, close to the long march, and formed on the left flank of the infantry, the whole line facing southward."

"While the English army went to these evolutions, the Highlanders showed equal promptitude and zeal for battle. As fast as the clans came upon the ridge which fronted their enemy, they were formed into line, so that both armies got into complete order of battle at the same moment. When this was accomplished, the Highlanders set up a tremendous yell which was reechoed by the heights behind them. The regulars, who were in high spirits, returned a loud shout of defiance, and fired one or two of their cannon...."

"The space between the armies was at times occupied by the partial and irregular contest of individual sharpshooters, and a hat or bonnet was occasionally seen to fall as a wounded man was borne off by this comrades. These, however, were but trifling skirmishes, for it suited the views of neither party to advance in that direction."

"Ere he could digest or smother the recollection, the tall military form of his late commander came in full in view, for the purpose of reconnoitering. 'I can hit him now,' said Callum, cautiously raising his fussee over the wall under which he lay couched, at scarcely sixty yards distance."

"From the neighboring hamlets the peasantry cautiously showed themselves, as if watching the issue of the expected engagement..."

"It was at that instant that, looking around him, he saw the wild dress and appearance of his Highland associates, heard their whispers in an uncouth an unknown language."

It's not too difficult to exchange words such as Government for Mexican or Jacobites for Texians and to wonder if Travis himself recalled any of the scenarios in the novels he read and made a connection. Of other Scott's works he may have read are such words as these from *The Vision Of Don Roderick*:

A various host --from kindred realms they came,
Brethren in arms, but rivals in renown--
For yon fair bands shall merry England claim,
And with their deeds of valour deck her crown,
Hers their bold port, and hers their marshal frown,
Their eyes of azure, and their locks of brown,
And the blunt speech that bursts without a pause,
And freedom thoughts, which league the soldier with the Laws.

In the music section of this book is a song entitled "All the Blue Bonnets" from Scott's *The Monastery* from which comes the Texas song "The Union Call,". It is described in Scott's book:

" 'Some one sing, if no one list to speak. Meat eaten without either mirth or music is ill of digestion. Louis,' he added, speaking to one of the youngest of his followers, 'thou art ready enough to sing when no one bids thee.'

The young man looked first at his master, then up to the arched roof of the hall, then drank off the horn of ale, or wine, which stood beside him, and with a rough yet not unmelodious voice sang the following ditty to the ancient air of "Blue Bonnets Over the Border": *

This song, rude as it was, had in it that warlike character which at any other time would have roused Halbert's spirit; but at present the charm minstrelsy had no effect upon him."

*(the lyrics are listed in the music section).

Travis also read Byron and Burns as did Sam Houston. Among Houston's belongings which he entrusted to Judge John M. Dor for safekeeping there was listed: one table and four chairs etc. and a library that featured ten volumes of Shakespeare, eight of Plutarch, his two volumes of Iliad, Burns and Byron. In several earlier biographies written about Houston nothing much is mentioned of Burns until James L. Haley, using new sources and newly released private papers reveals Houston's use of Burns poetry especially when writing to his son Sam Jr. Of course the evidence was there when he used Burns' words "Now's the Day and Now's the Hour" from "Bruce's Address" when calling for volunteers to come to Texas in October 1835.

Robert Burns, now the National Bard of Scotland, and writer of the world's New Years Eve anthem, "Auld Lang Syne", has had more of an impact than most people realize. His songs have been sung worldwide and in the Southern states his music was used to write songs from the early 1800s and on through the War Between the States. I have collected a half dozen or more songs written to the tune "Tutti Taitie/ Scot's Wha Ha'e", that sing of early Texas history. Tradition has it that this tune was played on the eve of the Battle of Bannockburn by Bruce's musicians as a stirring march. Robert Burns, on hearing this during one of his trips through Stirling, later wrote words to what he imagined Bruce might have said to his men that night. Burns visited Bannockburn in August, 1787, and in his journal he wrote, "here no Scot can pass uninterested. I fancy to myself that I see my gallant countrymen coming over the hill, and down upon the plunderers of their country, the murderers of their fathers, noble revenge and just hate glowing in every vein, striding more and more eagerly as they approach the oppressive, insulting, bloodthirsty foe. I see them meet in glorious triumphant congratulations on the victorious field, exulting in their heroic royal leader, and rescue liberty and independence."

Burns wrote the words on August 1st, 1793. Notes from *The Popular Melodies and Songs of Scotland* published in 1891 say it best:

> It appears, that on July 30th, 1793, Burns and his friend, Mr. John Syme, set out on horseback from the house of Mr. Gordon of Kenmure, for Gatehouse, a village in the Stewartry of Kirkcudbright. (says Mr. Syme) 'I took him by the moor-road, where savage and desolate regions extended wide around. The sky was sympathetic with the wretchedness of the soil; it became lowering and dark. The hollow winds sighed; the lightnings gleamed; the thunder rolled. The poet enjoyed the awful scene-- he spoke not a word, but seemed wrapt in meditation. What do you think he was about? He was charging the English army along with Bruce at Bannockburn. Next day (August 2nd 1793) he produced me the following Address of Bruce to his troops.'

The oldest song known to this air is usually called "Hey Tutti Taitie" and seems to be an old Jacobite song written after the rising of 1715.

In The Daughters of the Republic of Texas Library there is a letter from John Cross, a volunteer with Fannin's army, who died in the massacre at Goliad. It states in part:

> When money was liberally given the proclamation was read and an appeal to all true patriots to join them and some appropriate speeches were made tending to touch the feeling, when Lo, my heart responded to the call and I found as Burns says "My mother's Highland blood risings in my veins and rushing like a

torrent through my heart."… I immediately enrolled my name as a volunteer…

For many years San Jacinto Day was celebrated in Texas with more enthusiasm than the Fourth of July was elsewhere. The song of the day was "Texas Heroes" written to the tune of Burns' "Auld Lang Syne". He could not have known how his influence would spread. Around the world on January 25th, Burns suppers are held to celebrate his birthday.

George Gordon (Lord) Byron was not born in Scotland, but his mother was Scottish and he spent the early years of his life in Aberdeen, Scotland. He described himself as being born half a Scot and bred a whole one. There are writings of Byron that would have indeed inspired freedom fighters. To Lucifer in "Cain" he writes:
> Souls who dare use their immortality,
> Souls who dare look the Omnipotent tyrant in
> His everlasting face and tell him that
> Evil is not good.

And from *Don Juan*:
> For I will teach, if possible, the stones
> To rise against Earth's tyrants. Never let it
> Be said that we still truckle under thrones-
> But ye, our children's children! Think how we
> Showed what things were before the world was free.

Travis, in his journals, recorded the number of women he slept with. Surely Travis must have read Don Juan.

Gringo

A popular misconception is that the term "gringo" is derived from a song that had the words "Green grow the rushes..." which was sung by American soldiers during marches. The Mexicans referred to the soldiers as the men who sang "Green grow", which was shortened to gringo. Two songs are brought up as possible sources, one being Robert Burns "Green

Grow The Rashes-o", (often confused because of the title, dated 1794) but this song is in a slow tempo, not suitable for marching. The other song is "I'll sing you one O, Green grow the rushes, O". The earliest we could find this in print was in *English Country Songs*: Leadenhall Press, London, 1893, which would make it too recent to be heard in Texas during the revolution. Having dispelled with the song theory we also find the term was not in popular use during the Texas Revolution but more so during the Spanish-American war (1898). It was, however, used as early as the eighteenth century. Spanish historian, Terreros y Pando, in his dictionary, compiled some time before 1750 states that "gringo" was a nickname given to foreigners in Malaga or Madrid. Spanish soldiers sent to Mexico in 1767 were called gringos by the Mexican people but between the late 1760s and the early 1830s, little or no use of the word was found. It does appear in writings from South America also, during the 1800s. However, looking at the Merriam-Webster's dictionary one sees that the word is actually Spanish, derived from the Greek word for stranger. (Etymology: Spanish, alteration of griego Greek, stranger, from Latin Graecus Greek; Date: 1849)

Epilogue

The music reflects the people, and with this in mind we will notice that a number of songs in the music section are of English origin. We should therefore not ignore the fact that a large number of English immigrants were also escaping religious oppression and a large number of them were original colonists. This may be reflected in a passage from Henry Smith's letter to his fellow citizens of Texas, where he states:

> "The eyes of the world are upon us! Shall we disappoint their hopes and expectations? No; let us fly at once to our arms, march to the battlefield, meet the foe, and give renewed evidence to the world, that the arms of freemen, uplifted in defense of their rights and liberties, are irresistible. Now is the day and now is the hour, that Texas expects every man to do his duty. Let us show ourselves worthy to be free and we shall be free"

In this short passage we find a quote from Robert Burns' "Scots Wha Ha'e", and a quote from Lord Nelson, of England, at the Battle of Trafalgar, who said: "England expects every man to do his duty." It was on October 21st, 1805, that the Battle of Trafalgar was fought when Lord Horatio Nelson commanding the British Fleet met and defeated the Combined Fleet of France and Spain. Nelson was mortally wounded in the battle but it insured British naval dominance for more than the next hundred years.

Today, the Scots in America celebrate their heritage every April 6th (Tartan Day, since 1998), but Highland festivals, Scottish games, Scottish gatherings and such have been going on for decades, some for over one hundred and fifty years on an annual basis. The concept of a Highland Gathering is said to have its origins in the Highlands when neighboring clans got together on a friendly basis to compete in acts of strength or music. Today in America, and indeed around the world, this tradition has blossomed into a full blown cultural affair where some gatherings range from a couple of hundred people to sometimes eighty to a hundred tousand on certain weekends. The competitions now include dancing, piping, drumming, fiddling, harping, tossing the caber and haggis tossing!!! Some include Scotch whisky tasting and all include lots of good Scottish fun. They are held throughout the year in every state.

In Texas there are several Scottish Festivals including San Antonio's festival in early April, right after Tartan Day. In early June, the Arlington Scottish Festival takes place, one of the largest in Texas. The Salado Scottish Festival is held in mid-November on the farm once owned by Elijah Sterling Clack Robertson. Robertson was born in Tennessee on August 21st 1820. His father, Sterling Clack Robertson was born on October 2nd 1785 and in 1822 was one of seventy members of The Texas Association who asked the Mexican government for permission to settle in Texas. He was later credited with bringing 600 families to Texas. It was Elijah who founded Salado and Salado College. The Robertson family still own the farm today and run the festival.

Probably the best known of all the festivals in the USA is the one held at Grandfather Mountain in North Carolina. It runs from Wednesday to Sunday in July with a variety of events that also includes track and field as well as road races and a marathon. The Vice President of Operations and General Manager of the Grandfather Mountain Games is Frank Vance, whose 5th great-uncle is Sam Houston. Frank's mother is also a Houston. The founders of these games are MacDonalds, and the family still figures prominently as organizers and entertainers with names such as Flora and Jamie leading the way.

The Detroit Festival in Michigan held in August and the Pleasanton Festival in California in September have both been held for over 150 years and draw huge crowds. There are gatherings from Maine to Hawaii, Enumclaw in Washington to Miami Florida, even in Alaska. All across Canada, as one would expect, from French-speaking Montreal to Ontario's Glengarry games in Maxville and out to the west coast they celebrate their Scottish heritage. All around the world these gatherings can be found as well as Saint Andrew's Day dinners held around November 30th and Robert Burns Suppers as close to January 25th as possible. I must say through all my travels that I don't believe I have been anywhere or met more people aware of their Scottish heritage than the people of the Southern states of America. Scratch the surface of most Southerners and you'll find a Scot.

Now let the music reflect the people.

The Songs and the Music

The Album cover for Carl's *Scotland Remembers the Alamo* CD uses as its background the Texas Bluebonnet tartan and the MacGregor tartan. The colours of the Texas Bluebonnet tartan, a district tartan, are based on the bluebonnet flower, which is widespread in many parts of Texas. The flower changes colour with the passing of time, the 'brim' becoming flecked with a wine red color. This tartan has been accredited by the Scottish Tartans Society.

The MacGregor tartan represents the presence of John MacGregor, a Scotchman who played the bagpipes during the siege, and sometimes tried to musically out-duel a fiddler player, who may have been Davy Crockett. The images on the album cover, across the top of the Alamo, are: William Travis, Sam Houston, Davy Crockett, Jim Bowie, Walter Scott and Robert Burns.

The older pipe tunes and fiddle tunes used on this album were tunes that were known during the time period. I asked the various musicians who performed on the album to fill out their instrumental medleys with tunes that may have been popular or known in America during the 1830s or were at least written before the 1830s. We've taken the liberty of supposing that these were tunes that could have been played by MacGregor on his pipes, Crockett on his fiddle, or sung by the men of the Alamo.

Remember the Alamo

The collection starts with the song *Remember the Alamo* written by Jane Bowers. This song was written in the 1950's and was popularized by The Kingston Trio and Donovan. Jane Bowers was a resident of San Antonio, Texas, where she died June 18, 2000 at the age of 79. The tune itself fits perfectly to the notes of the chanter of the bagpipes. This song, although one of the most recently written ones about the Alamo provides a fitting introduction.

Remember the Alamo
Jane Bowers

The bravest of brave were challenged by Travis to die
By the line that he drew with his sword e'er the battle was nigh
The man who would fight till his death cross over
But he who would live better fly
And on that day died one hundred and eighty nine

Chorus
Hie! up Santa Anna we're killing your soldiers below
So the rest of Texas will know
And Remember the Alamo

Jim Bowie lay dying his powder was ready and dry
From flat on his back Bowie killed him a few in reply
And brave Davy Crockett was valiantly fighting
The battle was fierce in his eye
For Texas and freedom were men more than willing to die

Chorus

A courier sent from the battle scene bloody and loud
With words of farewell, the letters he carried were proud
Fear not little darling my dying
If Texas is sovereign and free
We'll never surrender and always will liberty be

Chorus

"Ay, this was a day of cleaving of shields when a hundred banners were bent forward over the heads of the valiant, and blood flowed round like water, and death was held better than flight"
  - Sir Walter Scott, *Ivanhoe*

Hey Tutti Taiti/ Scots Wha Ha'e

The oldest piece of music on the album is the air we know as *Hey Tutti Taiti*. The air, no doubt, has an older name but the popularity of more recent song versions has long since extinguished all knowledge of it. The oldest known song to the air (*Hey Tutti Taiti*) seems to have been written after the Scottish rising of 1715, and before the death of Charles XII of Sweden in 1718. The most well known version of this song is *Scots Wha Ha'e*, with words written by Robert Burns.

In Burn's notes for *Scots Wha Ha'e*, in The Scots Musical Museum, he states "I have met the tradition universally over Scotland, and particularly about Stirling, in the neighbourhood of the scene, that this air was Robert Bruce's march at the battle of Bannockburn." Burns visited Bannockburn in 1787 but the words weren't written until August 1793. Regarding Burn's visit to Bannockburn he wrote in his journal "here no Scot can pass uninterested I fancy to myself that I see my gallant countrymen coming over the hill and down upon the plunderers of their country, the murderers of their fathers, noble revenge and just hate glowing in every vein, striding more and more eagerly as they approach the oppressive, insulting, blood thirsty foe. I see them meet in glorious triumphant congratulations on the victorious field, exalting in their heroic royal leader, and rescued liberty and independence." Mr. Lockhart, in his "Life of Burns," writes, "Here we have the germ of Burn's famous ode on the field of Bannockburn."

There does not seem to be a consensus on the spelling for *Hey Tutti Taiti*, it has been found as: Tuttie Tattie, Tutti Taitie, Tutti Taiti, and others.

The Texas songs using this tune, *Remember the Alamo* and *San Jacinto*, were recorded using just the A part of the tune, based on what was found in the books I used. It has since been discovered that this may have been a printing or publishing error, and that the two songs probably used both the A and B parts of the tune.

Hey Tutti Taiti
Traditional

Hey Tutti Taiti
Traditional

Here's tae the King, sir,
Ye ken wha I mean, sir,
And tae every honest man
That will do't again.

Chorus:
Fill, fill your bumpers high,
We'll drain a' your barrels dry,
Out upon them, fy! fy!
That winna do't again.

Here's to the chieftains
O' the gallant Highland clans,
They ha'e done it mair nor ance,
And will do't again.

Chorus

When you hear the trumpet sound
"Tutti taiti" tae the drum,
Up sword, and doun gun,
And to the loons again.
Chorus

Here's to the King O' Swede,
Fresh laurels croun his head!
Shame fa' every sneaking blade
That winna do't again.
Chorus

But to mak a' things right now,
He that drinks maun fecht too,
To show his heart's upricht too,
And that he'll do't again.
Chorus

ance: once
croun: crown
doun: down
fa': fall
ha'e: have
ken: know
loon: ruffian, villian

lour: lower
mair: more
maun fecht: must fight
tae: to
wha: who
winna: will not

Scots Wha Ha'e
Robert Burns, Traditional

Scots wha ha'e with Wallace bled!
Scots, wham Bruce has aften led!
Welcome to your gory bed,
Or to victory!

Now's the day an' now's the hour
See the front of battle lour
See approach proud Edward's power
Chains and slavery!

Wha will be a traitor knave?
Wha can fill a coward's grave?
Wha sae base as be a slave ?
Let him turn an' flee

Wha, for Scotland's king an' law,
Freedom's sword will strongly draw,
Freeman stand, or freeman fa',
Let him follow me!

By oppression's woes an' pains,
By our sons in servile chains,
We will drain our dearest veins,
But they shall be free.

Lay the proud usurpers low
Tyrants fall in every foe!
Liberty's in every blow!
Let us do or die!

ance: once
fa': fall
ha'e: have

tae: to
wha: who
wham: whom

Remember the Alamo

This song, to the tune of *Scot's Wha Ha'e*, was written by T. A. Durriage. Ten years after the Alamo battle the motto "Remember the Alamo" was still a battle cry for soldiers fighting to keep the southern border of Texas at the Rio Grande. This song was popular with General Taylor's men during this campaign.

When on the widespread battle plain
The horseman's hand can scarce restrain
His pampered steed that spurns the rein,
Remember the Alamo!

When sounds the thrilling bugle blast,
And "Charge" from rank to rank is passed,
Then, as your saber-strokes fall fast,
Remember the Alamo!

Heed not the Spanish battle yell,
Let every stroke we give them tell,
And let them fall as Crockett fell.
Remember the Alamo!

For every wound and every thrust
On prisoners dealt by hands accurst
A Mexican shall bite the dust.
Remember the Alamo!

The cannon's peal shall ring their knell,
Each volley sound a passing bell,
Each cheer Columbia's vengeance tell.
Remember the Alamo!

For it, disdaining flight, they stand
And try the issue hand to hand.
Woe to each Mexican brigand!
Remember the Alamo!

Then boot and saddle! Draw the sword!
Unfurl your banners bright and broad,
And as ye smite the murderous horde,
Remember the Alamo!

San Jacinto

The song *San Jacinto* chronicles Sam Houston's battle with Santa Anna at San Jacinto, once again using the popular tune *Hey Tutti Taitie* (or *Scot's Wha Ha'e*).

On San Jacinto's bloody field,
Our drum and trumpets loudly pealed,
And bade a haughty tyrant yield
To Texas Chivalry.

Our chieftain boldly led the van,
His sword grasped firmly in his hand,
And bade us tell the Mexicans
To think of Labordia

'Twas evening, and the orient sun
Into his bed was moving on,
When our young heroes rushed upon
The might of Mexico

Santa Anna traveled far to see
What man could do who dare be free,
In spite of Spanish musketry
Or Mexican artillery.

The boldest sons of Mexico
Have learned to fear a freeman's blow,
And dread the shout of "Alamo!"
For Sons of Liberty.

'Twas cheering to a Texian eye,
To see Sant' Anna's legions fly.
From Texas' dreadful battle cry
Of death or victory!

The carnage ceased, in triumph then
Proudly shone the Texian star,
And vengeance on her conquering car
Reposed most quietly.

The Flowers of Edinburgh

Susannah Dickinson, an Alamo survivor, recalls *The Flowers of Edinburgh*, as a tune that Davy Crockett played on the fiddle, with piper John MacGregor, during the 13 day siege. The vocal version started out as the *Flower of Edinburgh*, the song and tune appeared in Universal Magazine in 1749 and subsequently as a single sheet song with music. It became a popular fiddle tune played as a Scottish Country dance tune.

The dance music appears first, then the song follows.

The Flowers of Edinburgh
Traditional

The Flowers of Edinburgh
Traditional

My love was once a Bonny Lad,
He was the flower of all his kin,
The absence of his bonny face,
Rent my tender heart in twain.
I day nor night find no delight,
In silent tears I still complain
And exclaim 'gainst those my rival foes;
That ha'e ta'en me from my darling Swain.

Despair and anguish fill my breast
Since I have lost my blooming rose
I sigh and moan while others rest
His absence yields me no repose
To seek my love I'll range and rove
Thro' ev'ry grove and distant plain
Thus I'll never cease, but spend my days
Tae hear tidings from my darling swain.

There's nothing strange in Nature's change
Since parents show such cruelty
They caused my love from me to range
And knows not to what destiny
The pretty kids and tender lambs
May cease to sport upon the plane
But I'll mourn and lament in deep discontent
For the absence of my darling swain.

Kind Neptune let me thee entreat
To send a fair and pleasant gale
Ye dolphins sweet, upon me wait
And do convey me on your tail
Heavens bless my voyage with success
While crossing of the raging main
And send me safe o'er to that distant shore
To meet my lovely darling swain

All joy and mirth at our return
Shall then abound from Tweed to Tay
The bells shall ring and sweet birds sing
To grace and crown our nuptial day
Thus bless'd with charms in my love's arms
My heart once more I will regain
Then I'll range no more to a distant shore
But in love will enjoy my darling swain.

Dashing White Sergeant

A Scottish fiddle tune, *Dashing White Sergeant* was popular during the early 1800's, this was probably also in the Alamo fiddler's repertoire. The tune was composed by Henry R. Bishop (1786-1855), Professor of Music, variously at Edinburgh and Oxford. Bishop was born in Liverpool, England and is also well known as the composer of "Home, Sweet Home". It is unknown who wrote the words for "Dashing White Sergeant". Using this tune and slightly altered words a song surfaced under the title *The Female Volunteer for Mexico*.

The dance music appears first, then the song follows.

Dashing White Sergeant
Henry Bishop

Dashing White Sergeant
(continued)

Dashing White Sergeant
Henry Bishop

If I had a beau,
For a soldier who'd go
Do you think I'd say no? No, no, not I!
For a soldier who'd go
Do you think I'd say no? No, no, no, no, no, no, not I!
When his red coat I saw,
Not a sigh would it draw
But I'd give him eclat for his bravery
If an army of amazons e'er came in play
As a dashing white sergeant I'd march away,
A dashing white sergeant I'd march away,
March away, march away, march away, march away,
March away, march away, march away, march away, march away.

When my soldier was gone
Do you think I'd take on
Sit moping, forlorn? No, no, not I
His fame my concern
How my bosom would burn when I saw him return crowned with victory.
When his red coat I saw,
Not a sigh would it draw
But I'd give him eclat for his bravery
If an army of amazons e'er came in play
As a dashing white sergeant I'd march away,
A dashing white sergeant I'd march away,
March away, march away, march away, march away,
March away, march away, march away, march away, march away.

Female Volunteer for Mexico
tune: Dashing White Sergeant

Oh! I had a beau,
Who for Mexico would go
Do you think I'd say no, no, no, not I
When his rifle I saw,
Not a sigh would I draw
But I'd give him eclat for his bravery
If a band of young patriots should come in my way
As a volunteer for Mexico I'd march away,
A volunteer for Mexico I'd march away,
March away, march away, march away, march away,
March away, march away, march away, march away, march away.

When the field I am on
Do you think I would mourn
Or wish to return, no no, not I
With freedom I'd burn
All fear would I scorn
Till Mexico was crowned with liberty
If a band of young patriots should come in my way
As a volunteer for Mexico I'd march away,
A volunteer for Mexico I'd march away,
March away, march away, march away, march away,
March away, march away, march away, march away, march away.

Then arouse man and maid
Fair Mexico to aid
Grasp rifle and blade and never fly.
Till freedom again
Shall smile on her plain
Your life's blood drained for victory.
If a band of young patriots should come in my way
As a volunteer for Mexico I'd march away,
A volunteer for Mexico I'd march away,
March away, march away, march away, march away,
March away, march away, march away, march away, march away.

Bugle Calls

The bugle was first used as a signal instrument in America during the Revolutionary War. By the end of the Civil War the artillery, cavalry, and infantry were sounding bugle calls. The enlisted soldiers life was regulated by bugle calls: the daily routine included breakfast, dinner, and supper calls; fatigue call, drill call, stable and water calls, sick call, and taps. The Bugle Calls included here were for the cavalry, and were taken from *El Soldado Mejicano*. This series of calls are generally played in increasing tempo from the Marches, through Trot, and Gallop. From *Duel of Eagles*, written by Jeff Long, we learn that there were 70 bugle calls used by the Mexican Army, 57 common to both cavalry and infantry branches. The Degüello, music played by the Mexican army bands on the morning of March 6, 1836, was the signal for Antonio López de Santa Anna's attack on the Alamo. The word degüello signifies the act of beheading or throat-cutting and in Spanish history became associated with the bugle call, which, in different versions, meant complete destruction of the enemy without mercy, or "No Quarter".

Bugle Calls

Bugle Calls

Moses Rose of Texas

The tune used for this song is *The Yellow Rose of Texas* which was written before the Civil War, and was first published in 1858. This was originally a Negro song, and the "yellow rose" was thought to be a light-colored negress. There is also speculation that the "yellow rose" may have been a young, mulatto woman, Emily Morgan, that Santa Anna saw and admired. She was the servant of Col. James Morgan, but as Col. Morgan was away with his command on Galveston Island, Santa Anna ordered her assigned as a servant in his marquee, or presidential tent. The words for *Moses Rose of Texas* were written by Stephen L. Suffet, and tell the story of Louis (Moses) Rose who allegedly didn't cross the "line in the sand" and escaped from the Alamo the night before the final siege.

Moses Rose of Texas

Lyrics: Stephen L. Suffet, tune: Yellow Rose of Texas

When gallant Colonel Travis,
Drew a line down in the sand,
Everyone stepped over,
But one solitary man.
They called him Rose the Coward,
And they called him Yellow Rose,
But it takes bravery to stand alone,
As God Almighty knows.

He said, "I'm not a coward,
I just think it isn't right,
For me to throw my life away,
In someone else's fight.
I have no quarrel with Mexicans,
Nor with the Texans, too."
So Moses Rose of Texas,
He bid the men adieu.

Whenever you are up against it,
Pressure from your peers,
Or a challenge to your manhood,
Or frightened by the jeers,
Remember that discretion,
Is valor's better part,
And let the life of Moses Rose,
Put courage in your heart.

So shed a tear for Travis,
And Davy Crockett, too,
And cry for old Jim Bowie,
They saw the battle through.
But when you're finished weeping,
And you're finished with your wail,
Then give a grin for Moses Rose,
Who lived to tell the tale!

The Anacreontic Song

The Anacreontic Society was a popular gentlemen's club in London, named in honor of Anacreon, a lyric poet of Greece who lived in the fifth century B.C., and mainly wrote erotic poetry and drinking songs. Anacreon's work was discovered and translated in 1554 by Parisian Henri Estienne. By the 18th century Anacreon's poetry was so enjoyed in London by well-heeled fun-lovers that in 1776 they formed the Anacreon Society. Their aim: meet once every two weeks, get drunk, sing songs; it was the forerunner of modern glee clubs. Anacreon, the "convivial bard of Greece," became the society's patron saint. The society's membership, one observer noted, was dedicated to "wit, harmony, and the god of wine." The lyrics of *The Anacreontic Song*, were written by Mr. Ralph Tomlinson, who had been president of the society. There does not seem to be a single composer of this tune, but it was a collective effort by the members of the Anacreontic Society. John Stafford Smith (1750-1836), a court musician and member of the society, was probably the guiding force behind this endeavor and most likely is the person responsible for the tune as we know it today. Smith is also the composer of the British national anthem ("God Save the Queen"), the tune known to those in the United States as "My Country 'Tis of Thee". As early as 1798 the tune of The *Anacreontic Song* appeared in American papers with various lyrics. The most well known lyrics to this tune were written by Francis Scott Key in 1814, originally entitled "In Defense of Fort McHenry", the song became *The Star Spangled Banner*. This tune was used for both *Death of Davy Crockett* and *Texas War Cry*.

The Anacreontic Song

The Anacreontic Song

To Anacreon in Heaven, where he sat in full glee,
A few sons of Harmony sent a petition,
That He their Inspirer and Patron would be;
When this answer arrived from the Jolly Old Grecian
"Voice, Fiddle, and Flute,
"no longer be mute,
"I'll lend you my Name and inspire you to boot,
"And, besides, I'll instruct you like me to entwine
"The Myrtle of Venus with Bacchus's Vine.

The news through Olympus immediately flew;
When Old Thunder pretended to give himself airs
"If these mortals are suffer'd their Scheme to persue,
"The Devil a Goddess will stay 'bove the Stairs.
"Hark, already they cry,
"In transports of Joy,
"Away to the Sons of Anacreon we'll fly,
"And there, with good Fellows, we'll learn to entwine
"The Myrtle of Venus with Bacchus's Vine.

"The Yellow-Haired god and his nine fusty Maids
"From Helicon's Banks will incontinent flee,
"Idalia will boast but of tenantless Shades,
"And the bi-forked Hill a mere desert will be
"My Thunder, no fear on't,
"Shall soon do it's Errand,
"and, dam'me! I'll swinge the Ringleaders, I warrant,
"I'll trim the young Dogs, for thus daring to twine
"The Myrtle of Venus with Bacchus's Vine.

Apollo rose up; and said, "Pr'ythee ne'er quarrel,
"Good King of the Gods, with my Vot'ries below:
"Your Thunder is useless." - then, shewing his Laurel,
Cry'd, "Sic evitabile fulmen, you know!
"then over each Head
"My Laurels I'll spread;
"So my Sons from your Crackers no Mischief shall dread,
"Whilst snug in their Club-Room, they jovially twine
"The Myrtle of Venus with Bacchus's Vine.

Next Momus got up, with his risible Phiz,
And swore with Apollo he'd cheerfully join
"The full Tide of Harmony still shall be his,
"But the Song, and the Catch, & the Laugh shall be mine
"Then, Jove, be not jealous
Of these honest Fellows.
Cry'd Jove, "We relent, since the Truth you now tell us;
"And swear, by old Styx, that they long shall entwine
"The Myrtle of Venus with Bacchus's Vine.

Ye sons of Anacreon, then, join Hand in Hand;
Preserve Unanimity, Friendship, and Love!
'Tis your's to support what's so happily plann'd;
You've the Sanction of Gods, and the Fiat of Jove.
While thus we agree
Our Toast let it be.
May our club flourish happy, united and free!
And long may the Sons of Anacreon entwine
The Myrtle of Venus with Bacchus's Vine.

Glossary:
fusty: old-fashioned
risible : inclined to laugh
phiz : face
incontinent : lacking self-restraint
swinge : flog
fiat : decree
crackers: fireworks, lightning
Sic evitable fulmen: turn away thunder, protect against thunder

The Gods
Apollo - prophecy, music, healing
Momus - mockery (for Philadelphians: this is the god who gave the Mummers their name!)
Jove - light, sky, warmth
Venus - love
Bacchus - wine, gaiety

Death of Davy Crockett
tune: The Anacreontic Song

As a member of congress, Crockett had a hard time getting any bills passed. He generally sponsored bills that were not "politically correct", but instead were ones he felt were the right thing to do. As a result he adopted the personal motto: "I leave this rule for others when I am dead, Be always sure you are right, then go ahead." The phrase "Go Ahead!" became associated with Crockett through the media.

To the memory of Crockett fill up to the brim!
The hunter, the hero, the bold Yankee yeoman!
Let the flowing oblation be poured forth to him,
Who ne'er turned his back on his friend or his foeman.
And grateful shall be
His fame to the free;
For a bolder or better they never shall see.
Fill! Fill! to the brave who for liberty bled
May his name and his fame to the last---Go ahead!

When the Mexican leaguered thy walls, Alamo!
'Twas Crockett looked down on the war-storm's commotion
And smiled, as by thousands the foe spread below,
And rolled o'er the plain like the waves of the ocean.
The Texans stood there--
Their flag fanned the air.
And their shot bade the foe try what freemen will dare.
What recked they tho' by thousands the prairie o'er spread?
The word of their leader was still— Go ahead!

They came like the sea-cliffs that laugh at the flood
Stood that dread band of heroes the onslaught repelling;
Again! and again! yet undaunted they stood;
While Crockett's deep voice o'er the wild din was swelling.
"Go ahead!" was the cry.
"Let us conquer or die;
"And shame to the wretch, and the dastard who'd fly!"
And still, 'mid the battle-cloud, lurid and red,
Rang the hero's dread cry--Go ahead! Go ahead!

Death of Davy Crocket
(continued)

He fought, but no valor that horde could withstand;
He fell— but behold where the wan victor found him!
With a smile on his lips, and his rifle in hand,
He lay with his foemen heaped redly around him;
His heart poured its tide
In the cause of his pride;
A freeman he lived and a freeman he died;
For Liberty struggled, for Liberty bled—
May his name and his fame to the last---Go ahead!

Then fill up to Crockett—fill up to the brim!
The hunter, the hero, the bold Yankee Yeoman!
Let the flowing oblation be poured forth to him
Who ne'er turned his back on his friend or his foeman!
And grateful shall be
His fame to the free,
For a bolder or better they never shall see.
Fill! Fill! to the brave who for Liberty bled-
May his name and his fame to the last--Go ahead!

Texas War Cry
tune: The Anacreontic Song

Up, Texians, rouse hill and vale with your cry;
No longer delay, for the bold foe advances.
The banners of Mexico tauntingly fly,
And the valleys are lit with the gleam of their lances;
With justice our shield,
Rush forth to the field,
And ne'er quit your posts till our foes fly or yield,
For the bright star of Texas shall never grow dim,
While her soil boasts a son to raise rifle or limb.

Rush forth to the lines, then, these hirelings to meet,
Our lives and our homes we will yield unto no man.
Death! death, on free soil we'll willingly meet,
Ere our free temple's soiled by the feet of the foeman;
Grasp rifle and blade,
With hearts undismayed,
And swear by the temple brave Houston has made,
That the bright star of Texas shall never be dim,
While her soil boasts a son to raise rifle or limb.

Will You Come to the Bower

Santa Anna's defeat during the Texas Revolution came on April 21st, 1836 on the fields of San Jacinto. Before Sam Houston's advance on the Mexican camp he called for musicians to lead the soldiers. He was told they had one fifer and one drummer, and the drummer could not play rolls, could only beat out a rhythm. The tune that they played as they marched toward the Mexican camp was an old Irish melody, *Will You Come to the Bower*.

Will You Come to the Bower
Traditional

Will you come to the bower I have shaded for you?
You bed shall be of roses, bespangled with dew.
Will you, will you, will you, will you come to the bower?
Will you, will you, will you, will you come to the bower?

There under the bower on soft roses you lie
With a blush on your cheek, but a smile in your eye.
Will you, will you, will you, will you smile, my beloved?
Will you, will you, will you, will you smile my beloved?

But the roses we press shall not rival your lip,
Nor the dew be so sweet as the kisses we'll sip.
Will you will you, will you, will you kiss me, my beloved?
Will you, will you, will you, will you kiss me, my beloved?

And, oh! for the joys that are sweeter than dew
From languishing roses or kisses from you.
Will you, will you, will you, will you, won't you, my love?
Will you, will you, will you, will you, won't you, my love?

Billy Taylor

Billy Taylor is an old Scotch ballad that appeared in broadside versions. There are many variations on the tune and the story, one in which the captain marries the heroine. In some versions the song has a chorus. Here we have combined two variations of the tune. *Zachary Taylor* (written to the same tune as Billy Taylor), is a doggerel (a light verse of loose, irregular measure), which was undoubtedly written by soldiers, and gives an account of Taylor's operations from the beginning of the war to the battle of Buena Vista.

Billy Taylor

Billy Taylor was a sailor
Full of joy and beauty gay,
'Stead of Billy gettin' married
He was pressed and forced away.

But the bride soon followed after
Under the name of Richard Carr;
Snow white fingers long and slender
A' covered over wi' pitch and tar.

She's buttoned on the sailor's clothing,
Dressed herself up like a man;
Awa' she sailed like a tarry sailor
All aboard the Mary Anne.

A storm arose upon the ocean,
She bein' there amang the rest;
The wind blew off her silver buttons,
There appeared her snow-white breast.

"Now," said the captain, "My fair lady,
What misfortune brought you here?"
"I'm in search o' my true lover
Whom ye pressed the other year."

"Now," said the captain, "My fair lady,
Come pray tell me what's his name?"
"Some folks ca' him Billy Taylor
but Willie Taylor is his name."

"If Billy Taylor's your true lover,
He has proved to you untrue;
He got married tae another
Left ye here alone to rue."

"Rise ye early in the mornin',
Early by the break o' day.
There ye'll see young Billy Taylor
Walkin' oot wi' his lady gay."

She rose early the next mornin'
Early by the break o' day;
There she saw young Billy Taylor
Walkin' oot wi' his lady gay.

Gun and pistol she's commanded,
Gun and pistol by her side;
She has shot young Billy Taylor
Walkin' oot wi' his new-made bride.

"Now," says the captain, "My fair lady
Come pray tell me what you've done."
"I have shot young Billy Taylor
Wi' a double-barreled gun."

When the captain did behold her
And the deed that she has done,
He has made her a chief commander
Over a ship and a hundred men.

Zachary Taylor
Tune: Billy Taylor

Zachary Taylor was a brave old feller,
Brigadier general, A, Number One,
He fought twenty thousand Mexicanoes;
Four thousand he killed, the rest they "cut and run."

Arista was the first that he gave "fits" to,
Just this side of the Rio Grande
Resaca de Palma and Palo Alto
Proved to the Mexicans they couldn't come to tea.

Matamoras he disturbed with American thunder.
He knocked their houses and soldiers down;
And when the inhabitants had knocked under
He struck up "Yankee Doodle" and marched into town

Camargo was the place he next went to;
The individuals there received him well;
They wheeled up their flour and their vegetables,
And other "fixin's" they had a mind to sell.

To Monterey then he turned his attention,
And ousted 'leven thousand, every mother's son;
When the Yankee nation came for to hear it,
They very much applauded what he had done.

To Saltillo town he made himself known,
And marched right in and made himself at home,
Until he heard the valiant Santa Anna,
To that place he had a mind to come.

Twelve miles old Rough and Ready went to meet him
At Buena Vista Pass they had a bloody fight;
Santa Anna and his army had a touch of Yankee mettle
That showed them "the Elephant" just about right.

In the thickest of the fight old Zachary appeared,
The shot flew about him as hot as any hail,
And the only injury that he received there
Was a compound fracture of his brown coat tail.

Long live old Zachary and his brave army!
Three time three! Now give them a shout!
to punish all foes whenever they are "sassy"
Yankee Volunteers are always about!

Freedom and Texas

Freedom and Texas was written to the old Scotch air *The Birks of Aberfeldy*, which first appeared in print in the early 1700's. Robert Burns wrote the lyrics for the verses of the Scotch version of this song. He tells us that he wrote these stanzas while standing under the falls of Aberfeldy, at or near Moness. (Scots Musical Museum (num113)).

Freedom and Texas
Tune: The Birks of Aberfeldy

Chorus:
Gallant patriots arm and out,
Raise banner and the battle shout,
The proud oppressor's force to rout,
For Freedom and for Texas.

Let not her freedom star so grand,
That caught its fires from our lands,
Be pluck'd by the vile tyrant's band,
But arm and strike for Texas

Chorus

When first out fathers beat the drum,
And struck for freedom and her home,
Then sons of France and Poland come,
To their aid 'gainst foreign taxes.

Chorus

Come o'er the despot Santa Anna,
Man's on her soil fair freedom's plan,
Up and drive his murderous clan,
Far from the shores of Texas.

Chorus

The Birks of Aberfeldy
Lyrics: Robert Burns, tune: Traditional

Chorus:
Bonnie lassie, will ye go,
Will ye go, will ye go?
Bonnie lassie, will ye go
Tae the Birks of Aberfeldy?

Now Simmer blinks on flow'ry braes,
And o'er the crystal streamlets plays;
Come, let us spend the lightsome days
In the birks of Aberfeldy.

While o'er their heads the hazels hing,
The little birdies blythely sing,
Or lightly flit on wanton wing
In the Birks of Aberfeldy.

The braes ascend like lofty wa's,
The foaming stream, deep-roaring, fa's
O'er hung wi' fragrant-spreading shaws
The Birks of Aberfeldy.

Let Fortune's gifts at random flee,
They ne'er shall draw a wish frae me;
Supremely blest wi' love and thee
In the Birks of Aberfeldy.

birks: birches
blinks: shines
braes: hills
lightsome: merry
hing: hang
braes: hillsides
shaws: woods

Uncle Sam to Texas

The origin of this song's tune, *Yankee Doodle*, is unknown although it has been claimed by England, Ireland, Italy, the Dutch and others. The tune did became popular as an instrumental piece, with British troops in Colonial times. In the Texas version of this song, *Uncle Sam to Texas*, "Johnny Bull" appears; he was often mentioned in songs of the Mexican War. It refers to England, and the fact that they were not very friendly to United States during this time. England had her eye on some western territory and did not want the US to continue its Western expansion.

Uncle Sam To Texas
Tune: Yankee Doodle

Walk in my tall-haired Indian gal,
Your hand, my star-eyed Texas;
You're welcome to our White House hall,
Tho' Mexy's hounds would vex us;
Come on and take some Johnny-cake,
With 'lasses snug and coodle,
For that and Independence make
A full-blood Yankee Doodle.

Chorus:
Yankee Doodle is the word,
Surpassin' all creation,
With the pipe or with the sword,
It makes us love our nation.

My overseer, young Jimmy Polk,
Shall show you all my nieces,
And then the cabinet we'll smoke
Until our eagle sneezes;
If Johnny Bull's fat greedy boys
About our union grumble,
I'll kick up such a tarnal noise
'Twill make 'em feel quite humble.

Chorus

If Mexy, backed by secret foes,
Still talks of taking you, gal,
Why, we can lick 'em all, you know,
An' then annex 'em too, gal;
For Freedom's great millennium
Is working Earth's salvation,
Her sassy kingdom soon wi come,
Annexin' all creation.

Chorus

Draw the Sword Scotland

The words for *Draw the Sword Scotland* were written by James Robinson Planché, a British playwright and antiquary, who worked with Carl Maria von Weber on the opera, Oberon. The music was composed by G. H. Rodwell (1801-1852) who was employed by the Adelphi Theatre, in London, where he composed and authored many show tunes. The song *Draw the Sword Scotland* appeared in "Collection of ballads, songsheets", possibly published in Edinburgh, by: J. Pitts, sometime between 1805 and 1840. This tune later appeared in "Kerr's First Collection of Merry Melodies for the Violin", published in the 1870's by the Glasgow, Scotland music publishing company: James S. Kerr. This tune was used for *To The Field Freeman*, and later was also used for a Civil War song that began "To the field Northmen, Northmen, Northmen"

Draw the Sword Scotland

Draw the Sword Scotland
Lyrics: James Robinson Planché; tune: G. H. Rodwell

Draw the sword Scotland, Scotland, Scotland!
Over moor and mountain hath past the war sign
The pibroch is pealing, pealing, pealing!
Who heeds not the summons is nae son o' thine,

The clans they are gathering, gathering, gathering!
The clans they are gath'ring by loch and by lea
The banners they are flying, flying, flying!
The banners they are flying that lead to victory.

Draw the sword Scotland, Scotland, Scotland!
Charge as ye've charged in days lang syne
Sound to the onset, the onset, the onset
He who but falters is nae son o' thine.

Sheath the sword Scotland, Scotland, Scotland
Sheath the sword Scotland for dim is it's shine
The foemen are fleeing, fleeing, fleeing
And who kens nae mercy is nae son o' thine.

The struggle is over, over, over
The struggle is over, the victory is won
There are tears for the fallen, the fallen, the fallen
And glory for all who their duty have done

Sheath the sword Scotland, Scotland, Scotland
With thy lov'd thistle, new laurels entwine
Time shall ne'er part them, part them, part them
But hand down the garland to each son o' mine.

To the Field, Freemen
tune: Draw the Sword Scotland

To the field, freemen, freemen, freemen
The foe now threatens fair Liberty's star,
Arm for the battle, the battle, the battle,
And drive Mexican proud invaders afar;

Our young child of freedom is calling, is calling,
For aid against a phrenzied and merciless foe.
Then onward for Texas, with valor appalling,
Let vengeance and freedom be dealt in each blow.

To the field, freemen, freemen, freemen
The bold foe now threatens fair Liberty's star,
Arm for the battle, the battle, the battle,
And drive Mexico's proud invaders far;

Come wave high the banner, the bright starry banner,
Your hearts will take fire at the Red White and Blue,
Quick, launch forth your thunder, your thunder, your thunder,
With Liberty's star ever valiant and true,

Then shall the foemen, recoiling, recoiling,
Retreat to his cavern, or sink to his grave,
And his boasting be silenced forever, forever,
As freedom's bright star o'er Texas shall wave

The Union Call

The tune used for the Texas song known as *The Union Call* was *All the Blue Bonnets are over the Border*. The original air of the song *All the Blue Bonnets*, is called "O Dear Mother". The popular song version appeared for the first time in Sir Walter Scott's novel *The Monastery*, published in 1820. The words were evidently modeled on an old cavalier song beginning "March! March! Pinks of Election" which we find in the first volume of James Hogg's *Jacobite Relics of Scotland*.

The Union Call
tune: All the Blue Bonnets

Arm, arm, sons of the union,
'Gainst Mexican tyranny;
Arm for the battle

Arm, arm, in gallant communion;
The drums of the foemen insultingly rattle;
Their sun banner waving,
Our Texas star craving;
False nations send soldiers and captains to lead them;
Raise loud the battle cry, Onward to Texas fly,
To give her bold sons Independence and Freedom,

Arm, arm, sons of the union,
'Gainst Mexican tyranny;
Arm for the battle

Awake in your halls where you freedom first courted,
And rush to the rescue by sea and by land;
Awake on your rocks where the eagle first sported
And drive every foe from a hold on your strand;

Up with your sword and gun,
Down with your Spanish sun;
Your bright star will light you where ever you need them;
From Sabine to Sante Fe,
Shout death or liberty,
Till all Mexico wears the bright stars of freedom.

All the Blue Bonnets are Over the Border

Chorus:
March, march Ettrick and Teviotdale,
Why, my lads, dinna ye march forward in order?
March! March! Eskdale and Liddesdale,
All the blue bonnets are over the border.

Many a banner spread, flutters above your head,
Many a crest that is famous in story
Mount and make ready then, sons of the mountain glen,
Fight for your Queen and the old Scottish glory.

Chorus

Come from the hills where your hirsels are grazing,
Come from the glen of the buck and the roe;
Come to the crag where the beacon is blazing,
Come with the buckler, the lance and the bow.

Chorus

Trumpets are sounding, war steeds are bounding,
Stand to your arms and march in good order;
England shall many a day, tell of the bloody fray,
When the blue bonnets came over the border.

Chorus

Santa Anna's March

Santa Anna's March "as played by the band of the Mexican Army on the field of Buena Vista on the night previous to the battle... This beautiful air was brought on by some Kentucky volunteers, having heard it played by the Mexican bands at Buena Vista, while on sentry duty." The engagement at Buena Vista took place in January 1847, during the Mexican Wars.

Santa Anna's March

Santa Anna's March

Santa Anna's Retreat from Cerro Gordo

Santa Anna's Retreat from Cerro Gordo "the subject taken from a celebrated Scotch melody as performed by the American bands on that occasion." The attack on Cerro Gordo began on April 18 1847, the Americans were able to envelop and rout Santa Anna's forces.

Santa Anna's Retreat from Cerro Gordo

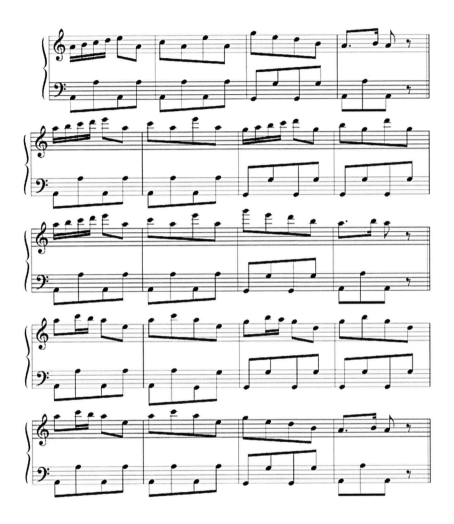

Santa Anna's Retreat from Cerro Gordo

Auld Lang Syne

Texas Heroes is a song remembering the fallen during the battles of the Texas Revolution, written to the tune *Auld Lang Syne*. The Scotch song has become a New Year's anthem all over the world. There is also a Civil War song written to this tune titled "The Lone Sentry", about Stonewall Jackson's sentry duty alone while his troops slept the night before the Battle of Manassas. For many years San Jacinto Day was celebrated in Texas with more enthusiasm than the Fourth of July was elsewhere. The song of the day was *Texas Heroes*. That it was written several years after the fact is indicated by the references to the abortive Mier expedition of 1842 and it's age scarred veterans. The glory of San Jacinto, however, increased rather than diminished with time.

Note: The word "syne" is often mistakenly pronounced "zyne", when it should in actuality be pronounced with a leading "s", not "z", the same as the English word "sign". The term "auld lang syne" translates literally as "old long since", and means "long ago".

Auld Lang Syne

Should auld acquaintance be forgot
And never brought to mind?
Should auld acquaintance be forgot
And days o' auld lang syne?

Chorus:
For auld lang syne, my jo,
For auld lang syne
We'll tak' a cup o' kindness yet,
For auld lang syne

And surely ye'll be your pint stoop,
And surely I'll be mine
And we'll tak' a cup o' kindness yet,
For auld lang syne

We twa hae run about the braes,
And pu'd the gowans fine
But we've wandered many a weary foot,
Sin' auld lang syne

We twa hae paidled i' the burn,
Frae mornin' sun till dine
But seas between us braid hae roared,
Sin' auld lang syne

And here's a hand, my trusty fiere,
And gi'e's a hand o' thine
And we'll tak' a right good willy waught,
For auld lang syne

---

auld: old
braid: broad
burn: stream
fiere: friend
frae: from
gi'e: give
gowans: daisies
paidled: paddled, wandered
pint stoop: pint measure containing two English quarts

sin': since
twa: two
gude willy waught: no expression of Burns has been more generally misunderstood than this. Gude-willie is a common Scotch adjective meaning good-will; its opposite, ill-willie, means malicious. Waught is a word in every day use for 'hearty drink'. The expression then, simply means a hearty drink taken with good-will.

Texas Heroes
Tune: Auld Lang Syne

We lay the crown of memory
Upon the place of rest
Where noble heroes lie asleep
Within earth's icy breast.

Chorus:
Then strike the harp for those who fought
For freedom long ago,
At San Jacinto and the Mier
And blood-stained Alamo.

For those who fell at Alamo,
And those who died at Mier
And those brave hearts at Goliad
All claim the silent tear.

On San Jacinto's crimson plain
Brave Houston met the foe,
And set his sturdy heel upon
The chief of Mexico.

When Santa Anna's star went down,
The Lone Star rose on high,
And blazed aloft a brilliant light
In freedom's cloudless sky.

Each veteran who stands today
Beneath the scars of age
Has made his name a shining mark
On history's living page.

For those who wear upon the brow
The crown of honored years
And those who bravely died we offer
A chaplet of our tears.

The Men Who Died at the Alamo
(listed by Birthplace)

Denmark
Zanco, Charles

England
Blazeby, William
Bourne, Daniel
Brown, George
Dennison, Stephen (or Ireland)
Dimpkins, James R.
Gwynne, James C.
Hersee, William Daniel
Nowlan, James
Sewell, Marcus L.
Starr, Richard
Stewart, James E.
Waters, Thomas

Germany
Courtman, Henry
Thomas, Henry

Ireland
Burns, Samuel E.
Duvalt, Andrew
Evans, Robert
Hawkins, Joseph M.
Jackson, Thomas
McGee, James
Rusk, Jackson J.
Trammel, Burke
Ward, William B.

Scotland
Ballentine, Richard W.
McGregor, John
Robinson, Isaac
Wilson, David L.

Wales
Johnson, Lewis

Alabama
Buchanan, James
Fuqua, Galba
White, Isaac (or Kentucky)

Arkansas
Baker, Isaac G.
Thompson, Jesse G.

Georgia
Grimes, Albert Calvin
Malone, William T.
Melton, Eliel
Shied, Manson
Wells, William

Illinois
Lindley, Jonathan L.

Kentucky
Bailey, Peter James II
Bowie, James
Cloud, Daniel William
Darst, Jacob C.
Davis, John
Fauntleroy, William Keener
Gaston, John E.
Harris, John
Jackson, William Daniel
Jameson, Green B.
Kellog, John Benjamin
Kent, Andrew
Rutherford, Joseph
Thomas, B. Archer M.
Washington, Joseph G.

Louisiana
Despallier, Charles
Garrand, James W.
Kerr, Joseph
Ryan, Isaac

Massachusetts
Flanders, John

Howell, William D.
Linn, William
Pollard, Amos

Maryland
Smith, Charles S.

Mississippi
Clark, M.B.
Millsaps, Isaac
Moore, Willis A.

Missouri
Baker, William Charles M.
Butler, George, D.
Clark, Charles Henry
Cottle, George Washington
Day, Jerry C.
Tumlinson, George W.

North Carolina
Autry, Micajah
Floyd, Dolphin Ward
Parks, William
Scurlock, Mial
Smith, Joshua G.
Thomson, John W.
Wright, Claiborne

New Hampshire
Cochran, Robert E.

New Jersey
Stockton, Richard L.

New York
Cunningham, Robert
Dewall, Lewis
Evans, Samuel B.
Forsyth, John Hubbard
Jones, John
Tylee, James

131

Ohio
Harrison, William B
Holland, Tapley
Musselman, Robert
Rose, James M.

Pennsylvania
Ballentine, John J.
Brown, James
Cain, John
Crossman, Robert
Cummings, David P.
Hannum, James
Holloway, Samuel
Jennings, Gordon C.
Johnson, William
Kimbell, George C.
McDowell, William
Reynolds, John Purdy
Thruston, John, M.
Williamson, Hiram James
Wilson, John

Rhode Island
Martin, Albert

South Carolina
Bonham, James Butler
Crawford, Lemuel
Neggan, George
Nelson, Edward
Nelson, George
Simmons, Cleveland Kinlock
Travis, William Barret

Tennessee
Bayliss, Joseph
Blair, John
Blair, Samuel
Bowman, Jesse B.
Campbell, Robert
Crockett, David
Daymon, Squire
Dearduff, William
Dickinson, Almeron
Dillard, John Henry
Ewing, James L.
Garrett, James Girard
Harrison, Andrew Jackson
Hays, John M.
Heiskell, Charles M.
Marshall, William
McCoy, Jesse
McKinney, Robert
Miller, Thomas R.
Mills, William
Nelson, Andrew M.
Robertson, James Waters
Summerlin, A. Spain
Summers, William E.
Taylor, Edward
Taylor, George
Taylor, James
Taylor, William
Walker, Asa
Walker, Jacob

Texas
Abamillo, Juan
Badillo, Juan A.
Espalier, Carlos
Esparza, Gregorio
Fuentes, Antonio
Guerrero, José María
Jimenes (Ximenes), Damacio
King, William Philip
Losoya, Toribio
Nava, Andrés
Perry, Richardson

Virginia
Allen, Robert
Baugh, John J.
Carey, William R.
Garnett, William
Goodrich, John C.
Herndon, Patrick Henry
Kenney, James
Lewis, William Irvine
Lightfoot, William J.
Mitchusson, Edward F.
Moore, Robert B.
Northcross, James

Vermont
Andross, Miles DeForrest

Unknown
Brown, Robert
Day, Freeman H.K.
Fishbaugh, William
Garvin, John E.
George, James
McCafferty, Edward
Main, George Washington
Mitchell, Edwin T.
Mitchell, Napoleon B.
Pagan, George
Parker, Christopher Adam
Roberts, Thomas H.
Smith, Andrew H.
Smith, William H.
Sutherland, William DePriest
Warnell, Henry
White, Robert
Wills, William
Wolf, Anthony

Unknown
John

Texas History Time Line

1716-1789 -- Throughout the 18th century, Spain established Catholic missions in Texas, and along with the missions, the towns of San Antonio, Goliad and Nacogdoches.

8 August 1812 -- About 130-men strong, the Gutierrez-Magee Expedition crossed the Sabine from Louisiana in a rebel movement against Spanish rule in Texas.

3 January 1823 -- Stephen F. Austin received a grant from the Mexican government and began colonization in the region of the Brazos River.

Mid-1824 -- The Constitution of 1824 gave Mexico a republican form of government. It failed, however, to define the rights of the states within the republic, including Texas.

6 April 1830 --Relations between the Texans and Mexico reached a new low when Mexico forbid further emigration into Texas by settlers from the United States.

26 June 1832 --The Battle of Velasco resulted in the first casualties in Texas' relations with Mexico. After several days of fighting, the Mexicans under Domingo de Ugartechea were forced to surrender for lack of ammunition.

1832-1833 -- The Convention of 1832 and the Convention of 1833 in Texas were triggered by growing dissatisfaction among the settlements with the policies of the government in Mexico City.

2 October 1835 -- Texans repulsed a detachment of Mexican cavalry at the Battle of Gonzales. The revolution began.

9 October 1835 -- The Goliad Campaign of 1835 ended when George Collingsworth, Ben Milam, and forty-nine other Texans stormed the presidio at Goliad and a small detachment of Mexican defenders.

28 October 1835 -- Jim Bowie, James Fannin and 90 Texans defeated 450 Mexicans at the Battle of Concepcion, near San Antonio.

3 November 1835 -- The Consultation met to consider options for more autonomous rule for Texas. A document known as the Organic Law outlined the organization and functions of a new Provisional Government.

8 November 1835 -- The Grass Fight near San Antonio was won by the Texans under Jim Bowie and Ed Burleson. Instead of silver, however, the Texans gained a worthless bounty of grass.

11 December 1835 -- Mexicans under Gen. Cos surrendered San Antonio to the Texans following the Siege of Bexar. Ben Milam was killed during the extended siege.

2 March 1836 -- The Texas Declaration of Independence was signed by members of the Convention of 1836. An *ad interim* government was formed for the newly created Republic of Texas.

6 March 1836 -- Texans under Col. William B. Travis were overwhelmed by the Mexican army after a two-week siege at the Battle of the Alamo in San Antonio.

10 March 1836 -- Sam Houston abandoned Gonzales in a general retreat eastward to avoid the invading Mexican army.

27 March 1836 -- James Fannin and nearly 400 Texans were executed by the Mexicans at the Goliad Massacre, under order of Santa Anna.

21 April 1836 -- Texans under Sam Houston routed the Mexican forces of Santa Anna at the Battle of San Jacinto. Thus, independence was won in one of the most decisive battles in history.

November 1839 -- The Texas Congress first met in Austin, the frontier site selected for the capital of the Republic.

11 August 1840 -- The Battle of Plum Creek, near present-day Lockhart, ended the boldest and most penetrating Comanche challenge to the Texas Republic.

June 1841 -- The Texan Santa Fe Expedition set out for New Mexico. Near Sante Fe, they were intercepted by Mexican forces and marched 2000 miles to prison in Mexico City.

5 March 1842 -- A Mexican force of over 500 men under Rafael Vasquez invaded Texas for the first time since the revolution. They briefly occupied San Antonio, but soon headed back to the Rio Grande.

11 September 1842 -- San Antonio was again captured, this time by 1400 Mexican troops under Adrian Woll. Again the Mexicans retreated, but this time with prisoners.

Fall 1842 -- Sam Houston authorized Alexander Somervell to lead a retaliatory raid into Mexico. The resulting Somervell Expedition dissolved, however, after briefly taking the border towns of Laredo and Guerreo.

20 December 1842 -- Some 300 members of the Somervell force set out to continue raids into Mexico. Ten days and 20 miles later, the ill-fated Mier Expedition surrendered at the Mexican town of Mier.

29 December 1842 -- Under orders of Sam Houston, officials arrived in Austin to remove the records of the Republic of Texas to the city of Houston, touching off the bloodless Archives War.

25 March 1843 -- Seventeen Texans were executed in what became known as the Black Bean Episode, which resulted from the Mier Expedition, one of several raids by the Texans into Mexico.

27 May 1843 -- The Texan's Snively Expedition reached the Santa Fe Trail, expecting to capture Mexican wagons crossing territory claimed by Texas. The campaign stalled, however, when American troops intervened.

29 December 1845 -- U. S. President James Polk followed through on a campaign platform promising to annex Texas, and signed legislation making Texas the 28th state of the United States.

25 April 1846 -- The Mexican-American War ignited as a result of disputes over claims to Texas boundaries. The outcome of the war fixed Texas' southern boundary at the Rio Grande River.

25 November 1850 -- In a plan to settle boundary disputes and pay her public debt, Texas relinquished about one-third of her territory in the Compromise of 1850, in exchange for $10,000,000 from the United States.

May 1852 -- The first Lone Star State Fair in Corpus Christi symbolized a period of relative prosperity in Texas during the 1850's. Organizer Henry L. Kinney persuaded Dr. Ashbel Smith to be the fair's manager.

1 February 1861 -- Texas seceded from the Federal Union following a 171 to 6 vote by the Secession Convention. Governor Sam Houston was one of a small minority opposed to secession.

13 May 1865 -- The last land engagement of the Civil War was fought at the Battle of Palmito Ranch in far south Texas, more than a month after Gen. Lee's surrender at Appomattox, VA.

1866 -- The abundance of longhorn cattle in south Texas and the return of Confederate soldiers to a poor reconstruction economy marked the beginning of the era of Texas trail drives to northern markets.

30 March 1870 -- The United States Congress readmitted Texas into the Union. Reconstruction continued, however, for another four years.

17 January 1874 -- Coke-Davis Dispute ended peacefully in Austin as E. J. Davis relinquished the governor's office. Richard Coke began a democratic party dynasty in Texas that continued unbroken for over 100 years.

Texas History Timeline is used courtesy of Lone Star Junction, Fairfax, VA (http://www.lsjunction.com)

Bibliography

Blind Harry, *The Wallace*, Cannongate Books, 2003

Blind Harry, *Wallace*, William Hamilton of Gilbertfield (translation), Edinburgh. Luath Press, 1998

Baugh, Virgil E., *Rendevous at the Alamo: Highlights in the lives of Bowie, Crockett and Travis*. Lincoln, NE: University of Nebraska Press, 1960

Bruce, Duncan A., *The Mark of the Scots*. Carol Publishing Group, 1996

Burns, Robert, *The Complete Works*. New York, NY, E.R Dumont, Calder, Angus, Byron and Scotland, Edinburgh: Edinburgh University Press. 1989.

Chariton, Wallace O., *100 Days in Texas: The Alamo Letters*. Plano, TX: Woodward Publishing, Inc, 1990

Chariton, Wallace O., *Exploring the Alamo Legends*. Plano, TX: Woodward Publishing, Inc, 1992

Crockett, David, *A Narrative of the Life of David Crockett*. Lincoln, NE: University of Nebraska Press, 1987 (1834)

Daiches, David, *Scotch Whisky: Its Past and Present*, Edinburgh. Birlinn Ltd, 1995

Daniels, George G., ed. *The Texans*. Alexandria, VA: Time-Life Books, Inc. , 1975

Davis, William C., *Three Roads to the Alamo: The Lives and Fortunes of David Crockett, James Bowie and William Barrett Travis*. New York, NY: HarperCollins Publishers, Inc, 1998

Dolph, Edward Arthur, *Sound Off: Soldier Songs from Yankee Doodle to Parley Voo*, New York, NY. Cosmopolitan Book Corp, 1929

Dow, David, *Greenock*, Greenock Corporation, 1975

Drummond, Ellen, *Emigration From Greenock and the Clyde*. Greenock, Inverclyde Initiative, 1985

Edmondson, J. R., *The Alamo Story: From Early History to Current Conflicts*. Plano, TX: Republic of Texas Press, 2000

Fischer, David Hackett, *Albion's Seed: Four British Folkways in America*. New York, NY: Oxford University Press, 1989

Fry, Plantagenet Somerset, *The Kings & Queens of England & Scotland*. London: Guild Publishing, 1990

Grant, Mrs., *Memoirs of An American Lady*. New York, NY: D. Appleton & Co, 1846

Groneman, Bill, *Alamo Defenders*. Austin, TX: Eakin Press, 1990

Groneman, Bill, *Eyewitness to the Alamo*. Plano, TX: Republic of Texas Press, 1996

Haley, James L, *Sam Houston*. Norman, OK: University of Oklahoma Press, 2002

Jackson, Ron, *Alamo Legacy: Alamo Descendants Remember the Alamo*. Austin, TX: Eakin Press, 1997

James, Lawrence, The *Rise and Fall of the British Empire*. New York, NY: St Martin's Griffin, 1997

James, Marquis, *The Raven: A Biography of Sam Houston*. Austin, TX: University of Texas Press, 1989 (from 1929 edition)

Keay, John & Julia, *Collins Encyclopedia of Scotland*. London: Harper Collins, 1994.

King, C Richard, *Susanna Dickinson: Messanger of the Alamo*. Austin, TX, Shoal Creek Publishers, Inc., 1976

Leckie, Robert, *From Sea to Shining Sea*. New York, NY: HarperCollins Publishers, Inc, 1993

Leyburn, James G., *The Scotch-Irish: A Social History*. Chapel Hill, NC: The University of North Carolina Press, 1962

Lindley, Thomas Ricks, *Alamo Traces: New Evidence and New Conclusions*. Lanham, MD: Republic of Texas Press, 2003

Long, Jeff, *Duel of Eagles: The Mexican and U.S. Fight for the Alamo*. New York, NY: William Morrow and Company, Inc, 1990

Lord, Walter, *A Time To Stand: A Chronicle of the Valiant Battle at the Alamo*. New York, NY: Bonanza Books, 1987

Macgregor, Forbes, *Clan Gregor*. Edinburgh: Clan Gregor Society, 1977

Mackenzie, A. C., et al, *The Popular Songs & Melodies of Scotland*. Glasgow: Bayley &Ferguson, 1891

Matovina, Timothy M., The *Alamo Remembered: Tejano Accounts and Perspectives*. Austin. TX: University of Texas Press, 1995

Prebble, John, *Culloden*. Penguin Books, 1966

Prebble, John, *Darien: The Scottish Dream of Empire*. Edinburgh: Birlinn Ltd., 1968.

Prebble, John, *Glencoe*. Penguin Books, 1967

Prebble, John, *The Highland Clearances*. Penguin Books, 1963

Prebble, John, *The Lion in the North*. Penguin Books, 1971

Ray, Celeste, Highland *Heritage: Scottish Americans in the American South*. Chapel Hill,NC: The University of North Carolina Press, 2001

Rios, John F., ed. *Readings on The Alamo*. New York, NY: Vantage Press, 1987
Ross, David, Scotland: History of a Nation. London Books, 1998

Ross, Stewart, *The Stewart Dynasty*. Thomas and Lochar, 1993.

Rough and Ready Songster, N.Y. & St. Louis: Nafis & Cornish, n.d. (1848)

Scott, Sir Walter, *Ivanhoe*, New York, NY: Nottingham Society, 1892

Scott, Sir Walter, *Rob Roy*, New York, NY: Nottingham Society, 1892

Scott, Sir Walter, *Scott's Poetical Works*. London: Routledge and Sons, 1887.

Scott, Sir Walter, *The Monastery*. New York, NY: The Nottingham Society, 1892.

Scott, Sir Walter, *Waverley*. New York, NY: The Nottingham Society, 1892.

Stewart, Col. David, *Sketches of the Highlanders of Scotland*. Edinburgh: John Donald Publishers, Ltd., 1877

Tinkle, Lon, *The Alamo*. New York, NY: McGraw-Hill Book Company, 1958

Wisehart, M. K., *Sam Houston: American Giant*. Washington: Robert B Luce, Inc, 1962

Carl Peterson's double CD, *Scotland Remembers the Alamo*, and this book, *Now's the Day and Now's the Hour*, can be purchased from:

www.darachweb.com
www.carl-peterson.com
www.DreamCatcherPublishing.net

Darach Recordings
P.O. Box 341
Kutztown, PA 19530
Phone: 1-800-279-2678

Dream Catcher Publishing, Inc.
P.O. Box 33883
Decatur, Georgia 30033
Fax: 888-771-2800